The Florida A&M University
School of Business and Industry

SBI: The Sybil Collins Mobley Years

A Historical Perspective of the
School of Business and Industry
from inception to 2003

Annette Singleton Jackson, Ph.D.
and
Leedell W. Neyland, Ph.D.

The Florida A&M University Foundation
ISBN-13: 978-0615882895
ISBN-10: 0615882897

DEDICATION

Force: *n*, /fɔːs/ an influence tending to change the motion of a body or produce motion or stress in a stationary body

$$\vec{F} = m\vec{a}$$

This book is dedicated to The SBI Force, a group of Superstar achievers so diverse and so powerful that none of us has yet imagined their total impact on the business world; past, current, and future.

This book is also dedicated to Sybil Collins Mobley and all those who have served on the faculty and staff of SBI. You have indeed inspired your Superstars to higher heights and equipped us with the pride, preparation, and purpose necessary to succeed.

Long Live SBI.

ACKNOWLEDGMENTS

Thank yous are in order for so many people who made this project possible. Dr. Leedell Neyland in his unyielding attention to historic detail is at the fore.

All photographs provided by Dr. George Clark, (Retired) Associate Professor and 3M Distinguished Chair, School of Business and Industry, Florida A&M University.

I must also acknowledge Dr. Israel "Ike" Tribble, Dr. Bettye Parker Smith, Dr. Lawrence Morehouse and the Florida Education Fund under the auspices of the McKnight Doctoral Fellowship for funding my doctoral education and introducing me to my McKnight Family.

Lastly, the dedication of many of my professors at FAMU; in business, economics, and all over campus helped solidify my standing as a Superstar. Further, the example set by my undergraduate faculty was so compelling, it set the stage for my desire for a lifelong career in academia. Though my father William G. Singleton, Sr. had long planted the seed that I could do anything, many of my undergraduate professors helped to show me how and added the means… I am therefore, acknowledging them by name:

Amos Bradford, Ph.D. Organizational Development
George Clark, Ph.D., Management
Rudolph Daniels, Ph.D., Economics
Saundra Drumming, Ph.D. Accounting
Charles Evans, Ph.D., Marketing
Emma Fenceroy, Ph.D., Mathematics
Larry Frieder, Ph.D., Finance
Clifford Marshall, Ph.D., Accounting
Leedell Neyland, Ph.D., History
William Ravenell, J.D., Business Law
Priscilla Slade, Ph.D., Accounting
Annette Tharpe, Honors English
Richard Wilson, Ph.D., Economics
Leo Upchurch, Ph.D., Quantitative Methods and Statistics

CONTENTS

FOREWORD

Dr. Leedell Neyland and Dr. Annette Singleton Jackson have done a tremendous job providing a historical chronology of Florida A&M University's School of Business and Industry's (SBI) origins, which includes the rise of Dean Emeritus, Dr. Sybil Collins Mobley. As young SBIans, my colleagues and I knew that Dean Mobley was a powerful, yet very special woman. She blazed unheard of trails for her day - for anybody's day for that matter. As a more seasoned SBIan, and now following in Dean Mobley's footsteps, I often say that "Dean Mobley is a woman way ahead of her time;" a true visionary (a descriptor that I do not use loosely). The pioneering business education program that she not only envisioned, but, more importantly, brought to fruition, is just as relevant today as it was the day she set the wheels in motion.

Dean Mobley had an uncanny way of mesmerizing people and getting them to buy into her vision. She would describe her visions with details so vivid that you could actually visualize things yet to come. But just in case you could not, she had replicas and diagrams of her vision created to provide you with tangible artifacts. One such example is the SBI Complex. As students, Dean Mobley would tell us about the SBI World Complex with an indoor plaza while we were housed in the SBI Building (now the South Wing). She said it would consist of four wings with a dome on top. She had a model of her SBI World Complex created. She would show it to everyone and describe the team rooms, classrooms, the presentation room, and other features in great detail. But not many of us put stock in her vision becoming a reality. However, when I joined the faculty in 1997, the second building (the East Wing) of her four-wing complex had been erected. Dean Mobley made a believer out of many because by the time she retired, all four wings of the SBI World Complex were erected. Although she was not able to have the dome constructed, she left us with the tools, vision, and desire to take SBI to next the level.

Dean Mobley's tireless work and relentless fight for her fourth child, SBI, has provided a buoyant springboard for all those who were/are bold enough to sign up for her "boot camp." Many of us did not like it while going through the rigorous process, but we can all appreciate the fact that we are the better for it after having gone through the program. Dean Mobley's SBI was designed to train an army of graduates that she said would be a "FORCE (SBI alumni) to be reckoned with," and that she did!

Our charge now is to continue the legacy that Dean Emeritus, Sybil Collins Mobley, Ph.D., started, so that current and future generations of students can reap the benefits and fruits of her unwavering efforts. Long live the best of all that Dean Mobley stands for and accomplished!

--Shawnta Friday-Stroud, Ph.D.
Professor of Management and Dean
School of Business and Industry

SYBIL COLLINS MOBLEY, PH.D, C.P.A.

1 FOUNDATION STONES UPON WHICH TO BUILD

The School of Business and Industry (SBI) at Florida A&M University (FAMU), in Tallahassee, Florida, is now recognized both locally and nationally as one of the most innovative and progressive business schools in the nation. Established as a school during the reorganization of the University in 1974 under the presidency of Dr. Benjamin L. Perry, Jr. (1968-1977), its first dean, Dr. Sybil C. Mobley, served from 1974 until her retirement in 2003. Under her leadership, SBI gained an international reputation for attracting high-achieving minority students, for its creative programs in academic and professional development, for its effective internship programs, and for its well-trained, racially and ethnically diverse faculty dedicated to implementing the ever-expanding goals and mission of the School.

The successes of SBI programs under Dean Mobley as well as its outstanding achievements in business education have been covered in numerous newspapers, journals, popular and trade magazines such as *Newsweek, New York Times* and *Fortune*. For example, a *Newsweek* (May 24, 1982) article, "Watch out Harvard, Here's Florida A&M," said that "by any standard, any color, FAMU students are superb." In addition, *The New York Times* (May 14, 1978) wrote: "Though the Florida A&M Business curriculum covers the same areas dealt with at most such schools, the program here has one feature of particular appeal to corporations...what the school calls 'leadership training development.'" An article in *Fortune* (December 28, 1981) stated: "Recruiters from such companies as IBM, Xerox, Continental National Bank & Trust, and Connecticut General Insurance have been tripping over one another in the hallways and the hospitality suites of Tallahassee hotels as they try to sign up students at FAMU's undergraduate School of Business and Industry." Despite these and many other accolades, Mobley readily admitted that the successes SBI enjoyed cannot be separated from the continuum in business training at FAMU, which began as early as 1915.

Over the years, SBI built on the foundation stones laid by previous generations who served when opportunities for black citizens were extremely limited or non-existent in the business world. The many successes of the School are owed in part to the developmental history of commercial and business courses at FAMU, which have been a formal part of the curriculum since 1915-1916. Under the leadership of President Nathan B. Young, a very progressive and aggressive academic leader, a limited program in business instruction was introduced in 1915 which included bookkeeping, shorthand, typewriting, and penmanship courses, which were offered primarily to high school students.

Within the next two years, the first two-year course leading to a certificate in commercial instruction was initiated. With very slight modification, the two-year program in commercial instruction was the principal program in business training throughout the 1920s. The purpose of the normal course in commerce, as expressed in the 1920-1921 *FAMU Bulletin*, was to "train young women for clerical and secretarial positions." Under the directorship of George DeCoursey, B.S., Florida A&M University, and Mrs. C. M. Bradford, such courses as bookkeeping, accounting, economics, shorthand, typewriting and business English were offered. All students were also required to take special training in penmanship.

In 1924, President J. R. E. Lee, a cosmopolitan and astute academician and administrator, became the leader of the University. In addition to his experience as a professor and administrator at Tuskegee Institute and Benedict College, he had served as the extension secretary of the National Urban League in New York City. The latter position enabled him to interact freely with executive officers from large corporations; therefore, he gained a wider appreciation for potential opportunities for well-trained persons in the business world. Consequently, one of his early emphases was to establish a four-year program in business. Through the influence of Dr. Lee, in 1930-31, the Board of Control approved a four-year curriculum in the Department of Business and Commercial Sciences leading to the B.S. degree. According to the *College Bulletin*, 1930-1931, this expanded curriculum was designed "to prepare students desirous of becoming useful factors in going concerns, to operate their own business projects successfully, or to teach commercial subjects in high schools."

The development of the four-year program owes much to A.C. Rucker, B.S., Northwestern University, with further study at Atlanta University and Syracuse University. He was assisted by Mrs. C. A. Daniels, B.S., Florida A&M University, with further study at Gregg College in Chicago and Columbia University. These pioneer instructors prepared students for teaching and for the business world through a variety of required and elective courses such as business economics, typewriting, advanced accounting, shorthand, business organization, business law, and practical-level business courses. Since racial discrimination and legal segregation prohibited whites and blacks from working together in an effective manner, the business curriculum at FAMU was geared toward training for black businesses or for teaching in all-black schools. Students who completed a degree in business had to verify their competence in spelling, oral expression, and writing. If they were deficient in any of these areas, they could not graduate until the deficiency was removed. Also, those planning to enter the profession of teaching had to demonstrate the ability to teach and conduct a classroom effectively as a condition for graduation.

To assist students in their overall preparation for their post-graduate careers, the Business Guild was established, calling all business students together for mandatory biweekly meetings. The *FAMU Catalog* for 1944-1945 states: "The Business Guild is composed of students enrolled in the Department of Commerce. The organization aims to promote programs which will stimulate keener interest in business activities and problems through lecturers, informal gatherings, and to promote collectively the social life of members." Lectures were presented mainly by the president of the University, the business manager, and individual black proprietors from the Tallahassee community.

Dr. William H. Gray, a young, dynamic, energetic leader, was named the president of Florida A&M University in 1945. He immediately set out to recruit highly trained faculty members and to upgrade and revise all college curricula. He recruited Professor John Vernon Anderson from his position as business manager of Bishop College in Marshall, Texas and charged him with the responsibility of expanding and upgrading the Department of Business and

Commercial Science, which was located in the Division of Liberal Arts and Sciences. Professor Anderson, who held the B.S. and M.S. degrees from the University of Pittsburgh, with further study at the University of Chicago, was the first person with a master's degree to head the department. Under the watchful eye of President Gray, Anderson immediately reorganized the department, changed its name from Business and Commercial Science to the Department of Business. He simultaneously recruited more, highly trained faculty members, and expanded the curriculum so that it would become a force in the development of black business professionals to penetrate the slowly changing business sector. While preserving and expanding the traditional and popular existing programs of business education and secretarial sciences, Anderson foresaw a future for moving many in his all-black student body into the then less popular programs of accounting, finance, banking, and management. Therefore, he added new programs to the curriculum in business administration and accounting, which required 124-130 hours for the B.S. degree.

With a strong academic and experiential background in accounting and management, as well as a strong aggressive personality, Anderson's vision was to prepare students to capitalize on opportunities that existed, as well as to penetrate areas of opportunities that had long been denied. It should also be noted that Professor Anderson began his service in the early aftermath of World War II. Although legal segregation was still a way of life in the South, the returning veterans, who had already held positions in accounting, finance and management in various phases of the armed forces, wanted and needed formal training in those areas. Further, through the Fair Employment Practices Act, which mandated giving veterans preference for certain federal positions, combined with small gains being made in the private sector, Anderson's emphasis on more rigorous training proved to be almost prophetic.

The new baccalaureate program in business administration and accounting was considered relatively comprehensive for the late 1940s and early 1950s, yet it included courses that were practical in nature. The program included such courses as: principles of accounting, advanced accounting, principles of economics, principles of marketing, business organization and management, auditing, commercial geography, money law and banking, business law, consumer economics, and typewriting. Some of the above courses were also included in the Business Education curriculum to upgrade and strengthen that program. The two-year secretarial science program was gender-specific, indicating six hours of electives for women and six for men. Under Anderson, all areas of the department gained increased respectability as graduates were accepted into business-oriented professional positions in both the public and private sectors.

At the end of the 1952-1953 academic year, Professor James Vernon Anderson resigned his position at Florida A & M University to assume a new position at North Carolina A&T University in Greensboro, North Carolina. He was succeeded in 1953-1954 by Grace A. Curry Black, whom Anderson had recruited in 1951-1952. She received her B.A. and M.B.A. degrees from the University of Kansas, with further Study at New York University. Professor Black was the first member of the FAMU faculty to hold a Master of Business Administration degree. Professor Anderson had also recruited Lucy Rose Adams, who had earned a B.S. from Morris Brown, and the M.A. from Ohio State University, and Irene V. Mandexter, B.S. and M.Ed. from the University of Pittsburgh. He also had the assistance of Polly Fears, B.S., Hampton University and M.A., New York University, a longtime employee of FAMU, who had served in clerical secretarial capacities prior to joining the business faculty in 1948. The four years under the leadership of Professor Black, who became head of the department in 1953, did not witness any drastic changes in the Department of Business. While Black was able to upgrade the department with modern typewriters and business/office materials and equipment, there were few if any changes made in the business curriculum. Black resigned from the faculty at FAMU in 1958 to accept a similar position at Fayetteville State University in North Carolina, where she built a highly creditable department of business.

By the beginning of the 1958-1959 academic year, Dr. Lucy Rose Adams had earned the Ph.D. in Business Education from The Ohio State University. Her excellent background experiences, academic training, longevity of service in the department, and loyalty and dedication to FAMU, allowed her to be named head of the Department of Business. She inherited a Department of Business which offered the degrees of Bachelor of Science in Accounting, Business Administration, Marketing, Business Education, and

Secretarial Training. The marketing curriculum, which had been a part of the Department of Business, was deleted during her administration. She notified students and potential students that the program might be reinstated if enough students demanded it. Courses in salesmanship, advertising, statistics, investments, real estate and retailing were offered during alternate semesters to accommodate the needs and interests of majors. Over the years, business courses increased in enrollment, partially because liberal arts students had the option of earning a minor in business by completing 18 semester hours.

Under Adams' leadership, the curriculum in business remained essentially unchanged from 1958 to 1970. Even though new job opportunities were gradually becoming available to blacks in the corporate world and throughout the private sector, the business curriculum in the mid-1960s did not place major emphasis on these new opportunities. The *FAMU Bulletin* of 1966-1967 stated:

> The Department offers courses designed to meet needs of students who expect to enter some field of business or government service, to secure secretarial positions, to enter the distributive occupation or marketing research activities, to teach business subjects in high school and pursue graduate study. Courses are offered in the following areas of study: (1) Accounting; (2) General Business Administration; (3) Business Education; and (4) Secretarial Training.

Prior to 1965, the major emphasis in the Department of Business was on business education and office management. As opportunities for teaching business courses in the newly desegregated high schools in Florida began to decline rapidly, training and placement efforts at FAMU began to turn to business and industry. An increasingly larger number of graduates found placement in the 1960s in business, industry, and government agencies through the FAMU Placement Center and through individual efforts of professors like Dr. Sybil C. Mobley; however, there was no organized placement center in the Department of Business.

By the late 1960s, Mobley's leadership in accounting had become the dominant influence in the Department of Business, even though the majority of the state-appropriated human and fiscal resources were directed toward business education and office management. In 1962-63, the Department of Business had an enrollment of 180 students and awarded 28 baccalaureate degrees—14 in business education and office management, and 14 in all other areas combined. By 1969-1970, the enrollment had increased to 644 students with 68 receiving bachelor's degrees, 46 of which were in the areas of accounting and business administration. At the beginning of the academic year 1969-1970, the Department of Business had a total of 13 faculty members consisting of the following persons: Dr. Lucy Rose Adams, Pollie W. Fears, Evelyn R. Greene, Robert H. Hammond, Jerrylyne J. Jackson and Coreta L. Russell in business education and office management; and Viceola D. Blackshear (Sykes), Guy L. Darnell, Man Chad Maloo, Irene V. Mandexter, Dr. Sybil Mobley, Dr. Prabbu Naraim Singh, and Katie A. White in accounting and business administration. It should be noted that although business education and secretarial science had an enrollment of only 97 out of 644 students, six of the 13 faculty members were assigned to these disciplines.

2 THE BEGINNING OF THE MOBLEY ERA

Sybil C. Mobley became a member of the faculty of the Department of Business in 1963, chaired by Lucy Rose Adams. As an assistant professor in the department, she taught accounting classes while completing her dissertation for the Ph.D. in accounting from the University of Illinois. After receiving her doctorate in 1964, she assumed the leadership of the discipline of accounting, and immediately began to initiate progressive practices, innovative methods, and creative approaches in the preparation of young accountants which subsequently became the foundation for her nationally-recognized Leadership Program in the School of Business and Industry.

Mobley brought to the Department of Business an excellent academic background, exceptional self-confidence, a highly competitive spirit, a cooperative attitude, and an abundance of energy as she worked through her supervisors to upgrade and expand the program in accounting. A brief sketch of her early life and development and her subsequent achievements and accomplishments in business education and corporate America will demonstrate that she possessed and continued to develop outstanding qualities, so essential in academic and corporate leadership.

Early in life Mobley internalized the meaning of dedication, determination, confidence and commitment, and the discipline of accounting at FAMU sorely needed someone with these leadership qualities during the rapidly changing years of the 1960s. She was born in Shreveport, Louisiana as the fourth child of Melvin and Cora

Collins. Her father was the editor of the *Shreveport Sun*, a black newspaper (which the family still owns), and was therefore, accustomed to writing articles and editorials which challenged the status quo. Moreover, Mr. Collins was a political activist in the community and was respected as an influential change agent in response to city and community problems. Her mother was an elementary school teacher whose Christian missionary orientation always led her to be of service to others. Since both parents believed that black people must ultimately control their own destiny, they instilled in their children the idea that education was the key to more effective living. Although they lived in a racially segregated society which frequently oppressed and denied opportunities to its black citizens, Mobley remembers that her parents "tried to arrange our lives so we wouldn't be subjected to the social factors that would convince blacks that they were not equal." So despite the legal and social limitations that were placed on blacks, Mobley always felt deeply that she was equal to any man or woman, and could compete effectively when given the opportunity.

Mobley's early education did not follow a conventional pattern. Rather, her mother taught all of her children at home until they completed the third grade. Because of her young age of six and advanced grade level, the public schools would not accept her, so she entered the Blessed Sacrament School at the fourth grade level, later attending the West Shreveport Elementary School and graduating from Central C. High School. Upon graduation from high school, she entered Bishop College in Marshall, Texas and graduated with a B.S. degree in Sociology. Immediately after graduation, she received an offer to become a clerk in the Business Office at FAMU. Because of limitations placed on blacks by racial discrimination, black college graduates usually were forced to accept low level clerical positions. She had been recommended for the position by Professor James V. Anderson, who had joined the FAMU faculty as head of the Department of Business and Commercial Science. Mobley remembers that she was fascinated by the typing assignments on her new job, and enjoyed her increasing responsibilities in office management. At first, she experienced some jealousy and dissatisfaction from her co-workers over the fact that she was initially paid a salary higher; however, when her salary later influenced an adjustment in their salaries, she experienced excellent work relationships.

Between 1946 and 1960, Mobley served in various capacities in the business office and in the dining hall while also raising three children. She was married to James Otis Mobley, an alumnus of FAMU with both B.S. and M.A. degrees, who was a successful businessman, president of the State Business League, and a civic leader in the community. Faculty members and students were well acquainted with Mobley's Campus Cleaners on the periphery of the campus, and many students actually earned their way through college by working at his establishment. Otis later worked for the State of Florida Department of Education as an occupational specialist until his retirement.

While Mobley's children were still young, she gave up her position in the dining hall to begin graduate study with the goal of earning the doctorate. Her first step was to enter the Wharton Graduate Division of Business and Governmental Administration at the University of Pennsylvania in 1959-1960, from which she received the M.B.A. in December 1961. Her thesis was entitled, "Critique of the Current Status of Disclosure." She enrolled in the doctoral program at the University of Illinois in the fall semester of 1962, and received the Ph.D. in Accountancy in January, 1964. At the ceremonies awarding her an honorary doctorate from the University of Illinois, it was publicly announced that Mobley held (and still holds) the record at the university for having earned the doctorate in accounting in the shortest period. Her outstanding and thought-provoking dissertation was entitled, "The Implications of Giving Accounting Expressions to the Technical Coefficients of the Enterprise."

Upon earning the doctorate, Mobley continued her work at FAMU as an assistant professor of business and gave her wholehearted support to Adams in upgrading and strengthening various phases of the department, especially the program in accounting. Mobley passed the state examinations and became a Certified Public Accountant, becoming the second black person in Tallahassee to receive this distinction. In an effort to determine the relevance and effectiveness of the curriculum, she worked during the summers with various corporate and public entities such as IBM,

Price Waterhouse, Chase Manhattan Bank, Union Carbide, the Internal Revenue Service, and others.

As Mobley rapidly progressed up the professional ladder to full professor at FAMU, she effectively intertwined instruction, research, and professional services. Her insightful article "The Concept of Realization: A Useful Device," which appeared in the April 1966 issue of *The Accounting Review*, was subsequently selected for inclusion in a book of readings entitled *Accounting: Socially Responsible and Socially Relevant*, published by Harper & Row Publishers and edited by Richard G. M. Vangemeersh. Mobley's publications at the time also included other articles in *The Accounting Review* including "Revenue Experience as a Guide to Asset Valuations," (January 1967); "Measures of Income" (April 1968); and "The Challenges of Socio-Economics Accounting" (October1970). The latter article was selected for inclusion in a book of readings entitled *Accounting and Society* published by John Wiley and Sons, Inc., and edited by Ralph W. Estes. Another of her notable writings was "Accounting Education Zeroes in," *The LKHA Accountant*, Vol. *52,* No. 1, 1972. The quality of her published analysis and interpretation of aspects of the field of accounting led her peers to select her as a member of the editorial boards of *The Accounting Review* and the University of Florida Press in the 1970s. Subsequently, she served on the Boards of Directors of the following Fortune 500 corporations: Anheuser-Busch Companies, Inc., Champion International Corporation, Hershey Foods Corporation, Sears Roebuck and Company, Southeast Bank, Southwestern Bell Corporation, Dean Witter, and Discover Co. She had the distinction of serving on the Presidential Commissions on Industrial Competitiveness, and Minority Business Development, President George Bush's 1000 Points of Light Foundation, and for many years as Consultant to the Comptroller General of the United States.

In addition to her many accomplishments at FAMU and in the business world, she maintained affiliations with numerous organizations which include the American Accounting Association, Phi Gamma Mu Honor Society, National Association of Black Accountants, Institute of Internal Auditors, Florida Institute of Certified Public Accountants, and the American Institute of Certified Public Accountants. She also served as a member of the board of directors of the International Association of Black Business

Educators and the board of trustees of the Committee of Economic Development. She has been vice president of both the American Accounting Association and the American Institute of CPAs. In 1990, she received the Director's Choice Award which is given annually to outstanding women directors of Fortune 500 Corporations. In absentia, Mobley was also inducted as an honorary member of Alpha Kappa Alpha Sorority, Inc. Mobley also was a frequent speaker at universities, corporate groups, and at regional and national meetings of professional societies. Toward the end of her reign as dean, her messages were increasingly focused on SBI, its Leadership Program, and its methodology in bringing together human, fiscal, and physical resources in the education of quality graduates for the business world.

Because of her many accomplishments as an academic administrator and her effective interaction with the corporate world, she was subsequently awarded honorary doctorate degrees from the Wharton School/University of Pennsylvania, University of Illinois, Babson College, Bishop College, Hamilton College, and Princeton University. Further, she has served as special consultant to the United States Agency for International Development (USAID) in Senegal, Nigeria, Zaire, and Kenya, Africa, and served as a team leader providing consultant services for USAID to industrialists in Cameroon, Ivory Coast, and Liberia, Africa. Over several decades, Mobley's life and service had a tremendous impact upon business schools and corporate America. However, she readily admits that she considers the years between 1963 and 1973 some of her most meaningful and productive ones.

Building a strong accounting program at FAMU and sending forth highly qualified students to leading accounting firms and major corporations posed a Herculean task for Mobley and her small faculty. In 1963 and 1964, the permanent members of the accounting faculty consisted of Mobley, Irene V. Mandexter, M.Ed., University of Pittsburgh, with 60 hours of additional study toward the Ph.D. with a concentration in accounting, and Evelyn M. Hodges, M.B.A., Indiana University. Hodges, who was a CPA in the State of Indiana, also became the first member of the FAMU faculty to pass the CPA examination in the State of Florida, and reportedly made the highest score of all examinees in 1962. Hodges and Mandexter were both excellent teachers who believed in and practiced the traditional, classroom-oriented methods of teaching accounting. Commencing in 1965, Lillian Hines, M.A., served on the accounting faculty for approximately two academic years. Both Hines and Hodges resigned their positions and left the University in 1966.

Thus, one of the first challenges that Mobley faced was bringing together a stronger faculty to help her build a more innovative program. By 1970, Mobley and Mandexter had been joined by: Viceola D. Blackshear, M.B.A., Atlanta University; Man Chand Maloo, M.B.A., Atlanta University; Quiester Craig, Ph.D., University of Missouri, and a CPA from the State of Missouri; and John L. Green, University of Illinois, who subsequently became a CPA. In referring to her faculty, Mobley wrote in 1970: "There are only nine black Ph.D. / CPAs in the United States. Florida A&M University has two of these and is hopeful in its negotiations, which are now in process, for a third."

Following a pattern which was to be used widely in subsequent years, in 1971 Mobley advised the FAMU administration that she was bringing in Kenneth W. Perry of the University of Illinois as a visiting professor. Dr. Perry's visiting appointment was underwritten by the American Institute of Certified Public Accountants (AICPA), making FAMU the only university that year to receive an AICPA visiting professorship. During the same year, Professor Herbert B. Miller, partner, Arthur Andersen & Company, also became a visiting professor in accounting, as did Dr. Dee Keespie of the University of Arizona. Although Professor Guy Darnell (University of Chicago) was not a professor of accounting, his versatility and ability to effectively teach a wide variety of courses needed by accounting majors made him a tremendous asset to the discipline.

As stated above, by the 1971-72 academic year, Mobley had an accounting faculty which consisted of six permanent members and three visiting professors. Her emerging concept of leadership development for accounting majors which included thorough academic preparation, recruitment of high-achieving students, professional development, and selective internships placed a tremendous burden upon her and the faculty. Despite the demands of heavy academic loads, and other responsibilities, Mobley maintained that the faculty had distinguished itself in many ways, including: publishing in prestigious journals; appearing on regional and national programs of the American Accounting Association as well as serving on committees; serving on the editorial board of *The Accounting Review*, speaking at other universities and in community events, and gaining valuable internships at General Electric; First City National Bank, International Business Machines(IBM), Union Carbide Corporation, Chase Manhattan Bank, and Price Waterhouse. All these activities contributed to the growing excellence of the accounting faculty at FAMU. Also FAMU was the only HBCU with a faculty member on the national program of the AICPA in 1971.

Along with upgrading the faculty, Mobley insisted that accounting could not become a top program without exceptionally talented, high-achieving students capable of quickly becoming models of success in leadership roles. Unfortunately she did not find many students of that caliber in the Department of Business in 1963. Of the 180 students enrolled in the department in 1963 most entered through the "open door" policy which did not emphasize high scholastic achievements. So Mobley began a policy of selective recruitment for Florida students who were top scorers on the Florida State-Wide 12th Grade Examination. Through recruitment packets, telephone calls, and personal visits, Mobley and her faculty increasingly began to attract high achieving majors to the discipline of accounting. As a part of the packets mailed on a statewide basis in the late 1960s was a folio *"Choose Accounting... A 'today' Major"* and the new AICPA recruitment brochure, *"What's it like to be an Accountant?"*

Within a few years Mobley had developed greater interaction with the AICPA, "Big Eight" accounting firms, and other leading corporations. Thus, she began to seek their moral and financial support for her recruitment program. In 1970, Mobley was able to report that, "Last year we mailed recruitment packets to 325 senior high schools and 27 junior colleges in the state. Further, packets were sent to Newark, New Jersey; Shreveport, Louisiana; New Orleans, Louisiana; Los Angeles, California; and Philadelphia, Pennsylvania." A high point of the recruitment activities for that year may be seen in several 1970 documents in SBI. They stated:

> Last year, Peat, Marwick, Mitchell & Co. sponsored a banquet at the DuPont Plaza Hotel in Miami for outstanding seniors from the 21 high schools in Miami for Florida A&M University to recruit accounting majors. For

this effort, General Electric and Haskins & Sells made available graduates of our program who are doing well with them. This year Peat, Marwick, and Mitchell & Co. will sponsor similar recruitment banquets in Miami, Jacksonville, Pensacola and Tampa.

In addition to the recruitment patterns indicated above, Mobley and her faculty made personal visits to homes, advising students of the opportunities in accounting at FAMU. By 1970, enrollment in the Department of Business had grown to 746, with many high-achieving students who could successfully pursue a major in accounting or other demanding programs. These early years demonstrated to Mobley and her faculty that FAMU could not only attract student "Superstars" on a statewide basis, but on a national level as well. Mobley wrote of her recruitment program in 1969, "Our efforts indicate that our ability to interest high-potential students exceed our ability to provide the financial assistance necessary to enroll them in the program." Therefore, her next step was to more intensely encourage the "Big Eight" accounting firms and other corporate entities to provide more scholarship funds for FAMU's accounting students.

During the late 1960s, Mobley took a leadership role in placing high-achieving accounting students in "Big Eight" accounting firms, other major corporations, and in governmental agencies. She worked closely with the Reverend Clinton C. Cunningham of the FAMU Career Service Center in placing her students. Although the Career Service Center, which was established in 1959, had placed many business students in governmental agencies and with a few corporations in the 1960s, it was primarily through Mobley's leadership and interaction with "Big Eight" accounting firms and Fortune 500 corporations that they began accepting FAMU interns.

Dean Mobley remembers with great admiration, her first class of accountants in 1965, which included Yvonne Cofield, Loyce Grisby, Noble Sissle, Jr., Theodore Scott, Margaret McGowan, Lamar Suns, and Nathaniel Wesley. In many ways, these accountant graduates blazed trails for others, and demonstrated to Mobley the magnitude of the problems that black graduates in accounting faced in the South in the mid 1960s.

Nathaniel Wesley, Jr., who retired as an associate professor of health care management at FAMU, praised Mobley for her "ability to inspire confidence." In an interview on August 4, 1998 he stated: "Students who were most serious about their education at FAMU became 'baptized' with the spirit of Sybil Mobley who challenged each to strive to be the very best... Dr. Mobley's 'you can do' attitude was frightening to me at first as no one had ever expressed such faith in my intellectual abilities."

At Mobley's insistence, Wesley interviewed with Procter and Gamble in Cincinnati, Ohio, in the winter of 1965, and accepted a position there as an accounting trainee in the Comptroller's Division in August 1965, thus becoming the first accounting graduate from FAMU to be employed by the company. He accepted the position because he could not find employment in Jacksonville.

During Wesley's last year at FAMU, 1964-65, he served as President of the Student Government Association. He was an articulate, relaxed young man with graceful manners, whose interaction with William Baggs, Jr., Editor of the *Miami News*, led Baggs to write an editorial (October 19, 1964) about the plight in employment for black men like Wesley. He wrote:

> The young man wants to be an accountant, and you might think corporations would have their agents outside the door. But therein, one rub.
>
> He wants to go home, to Jacksonville, and be an accountant. That's all... He just wishes to become a skilled accountant... The word is plain enough that a Negro wishing to become an accountant in a corporation back home, in Jacksonville, is wishing for a thin dream... The essence of all this is that Florida is losing some of its most intelligent men and women.

The early interns who went to "Big Eight" accounting firms and to major corporations were, for the most part, breaking new ground. Not only did these highly qualified black students receive assignments in the northern, eastern, and western regions of the United States, but for the first time some gained internships in the southeastern region. For example, Lewis Davis ('68) interned with and later accepted a position with Peat, Marwick, Mitchell Co. in Miami, Florida. After an internship with Polaroid in Waltham, Massachusetts, Forrest Thompson ('69) accepted a position with Haskins & Sells in Miami. Thompson recalls: "All black accountants who joined 'Big Eight' accounting firms at that time were extremely limited and restricted in their assignments. The firms explained to black accountants that before they could be sent on assignment, the firm must call the clients in advance to see if they would accept black auditors." Thompson feels that FAMU students and graduates helped to desegregate "Big Eight" accounting firms in the South and made them more receptive to black accountants. Thompson, who earned his M.A. from the University of Illinois and passed the CPA examination in Florida, returned to FAMU as an instructor, and became the first black to receive a Ph.D. in accounting from Texas A&M University. After being a business school dean himself for a time, he later returned to FAMU and retired as an Associate Professor in SBI.

The young Mobley-trained accountants began to make their marks all over the country, and some, like Thompson, returned from the private sector to serve their alma mater. Saundra Twiggs Drumming ('71) interned with Coopers & Lybrand, P .A. in 1970 and was employed as an accountant with the same firm for two years before joining the faculty at FAMU and subsequently earning the Ph.D. in accounting from the University of Wisconsin. Dr. Drumming continues to teach Accounting at SBI as a tenured associate professor.

Clifton F. Byrd ('71) recalled during a recent interview that he was privileged to have two internship assignments during his preparation at FAMU—one with Mobil Oil in 1969 and one with Haskins & Sells in 1970. He indicated that Mobley and her faculty had provided him with the proper academic and professional development education to appropriately adjust and make contributions to both firms. Upon graduation, Byrd accepted a position with Haskins & Sells in Los Angeles for three years. Although the firm knew that he was well prepared and was considered one of the best in theory, he believed that he was restricted in his overall development because he was black. He was never given auditing assignments with firms or clients where his individual leadership abilities could be demonstrated, but assigned to group activities with brokerage companies such as Merrill-Lynch, Dean Witter, and others. It appeared that all black accountants during these early years were restricted to brokerage companies, non-profit organizations, or to a few companies which were willing to accept them in spite of their race.

Mobley continued to successfully interface with corporate America in the late 1960s. One of her early assignments in a "Big Eight" accounting firm was in 1969 and was arranged by William R. Gifford of Price Waterhouse & Company, headquartered in New York City. In a letter dated June 2, 1969, Gifford informed Mobley that he was delighted she would be participating in the Faculty Fellowship Program during the summer, and that a program had been tailored to best suit her interests. Mobley was to attend a mini training class for new staff members, Auditing Philosophy and Techniques, and to work and talk with partners in the office in Los Angeles "regarding various aspects of the practice."

Mobley was to receive a total compensation of $1,500 per month, a living allowance of $8 per day for meals and incidental expenses, reimbursement for round-trip transportation from Tallahassee to Los Angeles, and reimbursement for the cost of an apartment. This summer experience gave Mobley special insight into the operation of a "Big Eight" accounting firm that students in the business programs at FAMU needed more than a thorough knowledge of accounting practices and procedures to be successful in such firms. She realized students also needed specialized and developmental behavioral skills to enable them to adjust to the dynamics of the business world. This experience also formed the basis for what would later become a common practice at SBI: faculty taking internships or "consultantships" with Fortune 500 companies. She wrote an article in the Autumn 1970 edition of the *Price Waterhouse Review* which contributed to FAMU's emerging image as a unique school for the educational preparation of black accountants.

Despite restrictions on black accountants in most firms, FAMU sent forth a relatively large number of accountants who made their impacts felt throughout America. Although FAMU's records of graduates in accounting are far from complete, SBI has been able to assemble a relatively accurate list of accounting graduates from 1968 to 1980 which are included in the booklet, *School of Business and Industry: Past, Present, Planned, 1970-1980*. According to this document:

76 entered public accounting
30 were currently with public accounting
30 had earned their masters degree in accounting
7 were currently pursuing their doctorates
19 had passed the CPA exams.

On the basis of their experiences, early FAMU accounting students gathered, and with guidance from Mobley, sent an unprecedented memo to the AICPA with "Suggestions for Improvements of Black Accountancy" on March 11, 1969. Among the topics discussed were: (1) Black fellowships to attend graduate school; (2) Finance for student recruiters to return to their high schools and tell of the opportunities in accounting at FAMU; (3) Encourage public accounting firms to hire Black students for employment and provide internships with emphasis placed on firms in the South; (4) Sponsor guest lectures and seminars; (5) Place in the Code of Ethics a non-discriminatory policy; (6) Encourage CPA firms to sub-contract part of their detail work to Black student cooperatives; and (7) Include Black faces in AICPA literature and brochures. The memo also asked the pointed questions: "What does the Institute do for accounting firms? Is this done for Black firms also?"

The students specifically requested that the AICPA provide immediate scholarship and loan funds for both in-state and out-of-state tuition fees, and that it encourage clients to contribute to scholarship funds. As of 1969, the fees for resident students per academic year (3 quarters) were $1,340.00 with an additional $200 for out-of-state students. To further assure AICPA of the high quality of FAMU's accounting students they wrote: "our accounting majors are qualified to sit for all sections of the Florida CPA examination in May of their senior year." Shortly afterward, in 1971, AICPA gave FAMU $50,000.00 to support scholarship for accounting.

Mobley had interacted freely with Fortune 500 firms, "Big Eight" accounting firms, and various corporations and was an active and leading member of AICPA. She observed very carefully the problems and limitations faced by FAMU students on internships and upon entry into government, industry, and accounting firms. Mobley used her wealth of knowledge and experience to broaden the concept of a more functional Leadership Program for FAMU accounting majors and other business students.

As FAMU students were clamoring for more support from the AICPA for black accounting employees and interns in 1969, at the same time a group of black accountants in New York City were considering the establishment of a national organization that could deal effectively with the many common problems faced by the growing number of black professionals in the world of accounting. So in December 1969, nine black accountants in the New York area came together and founded the National Association of Black Accountants (NABA). The founders were: Ronald Benjamin, Earl Biggot, Donald Bristow, Kenneth Drummond, Bertram Gibson, Richard McNamee, Frank Ross, George Wallace and Michael Winston. The expressed mission of NABA was: "to address the professional needs which enable minorities to maximize their career potential in the accounting profession." Upon graduation, accounting majors from FAMU were encouraged to become affiliated with NABA.

By the beginning of the 1970s, Mobley and other black leaders in accounting had convinced the "Big Eight" and other firms and professional agencies across the nation that historically black colleges and universities could produce highly competent and competitive accountants for the marketplace who may be better prepared than those completing programs at large universities. Increasingly, accounting firms and professional agencies became more involved in the preparation of minority accountants. One such effort was a program June 4-9, 1972, sponsored by the Virginia Society of Certified Public Accountants and the American Institute of Certified Public Accountants at the Dulles Marriott Hotel, Dulles International Airport near Washington, D. C. This program was billed as "A Faculty Seminar of Teachers of Minority Accounting Students" and featured participants from black universities such as Howard University, Dillard University, Virginia Union University, North Carolina A&T University, FAMU and others. It also included major institutions such as the University of Illinois, University of Texas, University of Virginia, Harvard University, and other colleges and universities. Leading representatives from Arthur Young & Co., Touche Ross & Co., Haskins & Sells, Arthur Andersen & Co. and others also participated. Topics relevant for the times were discussed, including "Accounting education in the Black colleges and Universities," "The Cost Accounting Standards Board," "Faculty Internships in Public Accounting Firms," "The Development of Professors for Minority Students," and other topics of interest to accountants.

The last topic on the agenda for this seminar and the one which generated more interaction was "Should Black Schools follow Major Schools or 'Do their Own thing?" featuring Sybil C. Mobley of Florida A&M University. Mobley conceded that academic courses and subject matter contents should be essentially the same as that of major schools, but she did not feel that this alone would make black schools successful. As she stated in her presentation:

> Certainly, there is much in major schools that we should follow. We want our students to be able to land jobs and we also want them to be prepared to handle these jobs. To get the jobs, most of which are...controlled by the so-called establishment—our students must hold credentials which reflect standards set by major schools; but for our black students to be able to handle the jobs, the standards set by the major schools might merely represent the bare minimum of what we must do.

Mobley insisted that although students from black schools may be even more prepared than white students, growing up in a segregated and often racist society has robbed them of certain social and behavioral skills essential for success in corporate America. As Mobley put it in an interview with Dr. Leedell Neyland, 1998:

> They have grown up in a society whose institutions were structured to document their inferiority; these institutions which programmed their failure teach society in a very convincing way that they are inferior. This is only one side of the problem—a more serious and damaging part of the problem is that these institutions have taught blacks that they are inferior—and as teachers, we must deal with this.

Mobley insisted that our black schools and their faculties can truly change the damaging image that black graduates arrive at firms with severe handicaps. Greatness in institutions comes from their ability to demonstrate in the marketplace that they can send forth top products—the graduates. Harvard has long reached that level. "If a top student goes to Harvard and does well, the image of blacks is not improved. The student's performance will not be interpreted as evidence of what blacks can do, but that Harvard can do the impossible—teach the unteachable."

Mobley maintained that "Only when black schools with black administrators and professors start sending a stream of talent into society will society begin to doubt the inferiority of blacks." Therefore, black schools must establish reputations of quality, and they must develop a strategy to market our schools and let our many strong points be known." Mobley continued by emphasizing that self-image and confidence are the most important aspects of development for the business world.

She emphasized:

> We have the responsibility of convincing students that success is within their grasp...we should outline a career path for students and convince them that the paths are not mined with insurmountable barriers if they learn how to deal with mines. Let the student know that he's got the power. Give him confidence.

Mobley concluded by advising firms and agencies that when minorities enter the profession in substantial numbers, "these institutions and agencies will never be the same again." If the firms— i.e. industries, public accounting firms and governmental agencies are going to open their doors, they should not expect us to leave everything we hold dear outside the door." Mobley asked the question: "How black schools should be as black as white schools are white—. Our obligation to our students extends beyond providing our students with a bleach that is not toxic. We have got to protect for them those things which are theirs." While accounting students everywhere should know standard accounting and black schools should follow many of the programs of major schools; however, black schools must go further and provide for their students the social and behavioral competencies which are essential for success in the business world.

Mobley's experiences in corporate and governmental work and her emerging leadership in the AICPA, provided an appropriate background to develop a sound leadership-oriented curriculum in accounting which would better prepare students for the corporate world. Even though accounting was just one of several programs in the Department of Business, Mobley realized great success in the field of accounting where her writings and activities were having a significant impact. Primarily through Mobley's efforts, accounting programs at FAMU have been financially supported in varying degrees by business and industry since 1968.

The initial contribution came in the fall of 1968 with Union Carbide Corporation giving $1,000.00; Cooper & Lybrand, PA., $2,000, and Price Waterhouse Foundation, $3,000. The next year private contributions became even better. In 1969, Price Waterhouse Foundation made a special grant of $50,000 to help provide "catch-up" funds to permit an enrichment of the accounting program. This grant represented the largest grant that Price Waterhouse Foundation had ever made to that date. As stated earlier, the American Institute of Certified Public Accountants approved in 1971 a grant of $50,000 to FAMU to encourage further development of its scholarship program. Also, in 1970-71, Mobley was able to report that the major CPA firms, including all of the "Big Eight" accounting firms, and some industrial corporations had contributed an additional $54,000 to the FAMU accounting scholarship program over a two-year period. Included in the above amount was a grant of $16,000 to support accounting students and the program of accounting. Grantors to the scholarship program by 1969-71 included: Alexander Grant Co.; Ernst & Ernst; General Electric Company; Gulf Oil Company; Haskins & Sells; Laventhol Krekstein Horwarth & Horwath; Lybrand, Ross Brothers and Montgomery; Mobil Oil Company; Monsanto; Peat, Marwick, Mitchell & Co.; Price Waterhouse & Co.; John Rather; Touche Ross & Co.; Union Carbide Corporation; and the AICPA.

Although FAMU was receiving increasing support from corporate America in support of accounting, the State of Florida gave only meager financial support. In an effort to overcome the financial plight of the Department of Business, students sought to raise funds through a statewide raffle. However, the proposed raffle ran afoul of the state lottery laws, which forced them to take a new course of action. The next alternative was for the students to make a direct appeal to the Florida legislature for support for the FAMU Department of Business. FAMU business students, acting on their own, requested and received a hearing with state legislators in early 1971 to relate the story of the success and emphasize the potential of the Department of Business. They advised the legislators that "FAMU did not want permission to be inferior, but the opportunity to be superior." Their persistence and determination so impressed legislators that Senators Mallory Horne, Tallahassee; Lee Weissenborn, Miami; and Wilbur Boyd, Palmetto introduced Senate Bill No. 524, and Representatives Donald Tucker and Miley Miers, Tallahassee, and Joe Lang Kershaw, Miami introduced a companion bill in the House entitled "An Act relating to the department of business at Florida Agricultural and Mechanical University." Stipulated in House Bill #888, which passed on April 8, 1971, Section 2: "There is hereby appropriated to the board of regents for the department of business...from the general revenue fund of the state a lump sum of one hundred and eighty-five thousand dollars ($185,000) for eleven (11) additional positions and related expenditures." The joint bills stipulated that this appropriation was to be over and above all other appropriations and future budgets would be required to maintain this level of funding. The bill further provided that "the request submitted by the University and the Board of Regents in the future shall identify what approximations will be necessary to maintain the program at this level of funding."

In the final analysis and with overall cuts in government spending, the Legislature actually passed a special bill that provided $150,000 for the Department of Business to support eleven new faculty positions. News media on the local, state, and national levels praised the students' lobbying skills. *The Florida Times Union* (June 29, 1971) stated that "the appropriation was entirely initiated by students themselves...at a time when Florida was cutting back in educational funds at all levels." *The Atlanta Constitution* (June 29, 1971) wrote: "The students persuaded a group of legislators to introduce the bill calling for the appropriation and appeared at the committee to testify for it." The students claimed that this support would force FAMU into the "Economic Mainstream." Although Mobley maintained that she was not directly involved in the students' efforts, after the appropriation bill passed, she wrote a special letter of appreciation to most legislators dated November 23, 1971 which read:

> Florida A&M University cannot with legislators like you, lose…There is no action that you could have taken which would have demonstrated to us in a more emphatic way your sincere concern for the economic welfare of blacks and your faith in the ability of blacks to support of the special bill for the Department of Business at Florida A&M University.

Since the BOR did not permit individual professors or administrators to lobby the legislature without permission, and since Mobley was seen as the catalyst behind the students' direct actions, she incurred the wrath of the FAMU central administration. However, Mobley was able to show that after this special bill was approved, over $2 million in private funds were given to the school. Also, corporate America responded not only with financial support, but with aggressive recruitment that rendered FAMU graduates among the most actively recruited in the nation. Notable among the responses was the establishment in 1971 of an "Arthur Young Professorship" at FAMU by Arthur Young & Company which provided a salary subsidy of $7,500 annually. FAMU was the seventh university to be so honored by the company. Others were: the University of Chicago, Ohio State University, the University of Illinois, the University of Kansas, the University of Michigan, and Columbia University. The special "set aside" appropriations by the Legislature for business at FAMU continued for several years despite BOR and administrative objections; however, it later became a regular part of the overall university instructional and research budget.

Mobley was destined to bring high quality and unconventional approaches to accounting as evidenced by the Auditing Course for the fall of 1970, which essentially featured a distinguished lecture series. The course was coordinated by FAMU Professors, Mobley and Quiester Craig, and featured such outstanding dignitaries/scholars as R. Bob Smith, Partner, Peat, Marwick, Mitchell & Co.; Robert K. Mautz, Professor of Accounting at the University of Illinois; Howard Stettler, Professor of

Accounting, University of Kansas; Joseph A. Silvoso, Professor of Accounting, University of Missouri; Felix A. Kaufluian, Partner in Charge of Management Services, Lybrand, Ross Brothers and Montgomery; Douglas R. Carmichael, University of Texas and Consultant to American Institute of CPAs; William L. Campfield, Professor, Columbia University; Jack Arrell, partner in charge of professional development, Price 'Waterhouse; and James Gallaner, audit partner, in the New York Office of Haskins & Sells.

The Auditing Course not only brought quality instruction and attracted attention at both the state and national levels, but it gave Mobley and FAMU greater national credibility and a better working relationship with some of the leading accounting minds in the country. Mobley was to build on these and other non-traditional experiences as she worked to design a more sound leadership program in business. The success of the auditing class so impressed Professor Joseph A. Silvoso that he wrote in a letter to Mobley on November 30, 1970: "I have visited many places in my life and my visit to A&M will always be cherished as one of my most pleasing experiences. You are, indeed, most fortunate to be located with an administrative staff, faculty, and students of such high caliber." He continued: "We are interested in attracting your students to study with us. I believe that we are able to provide an educational experience which will enable them to make an outstanding career in the accounting profession."

Subsequent to returning to the University of Missouri, Professor Silvoso, true to his word, recruited many SBI students—the first of whom received masters degrees in 1973.

During the 1969-1970 academic year, the chairperson, Lucy Rose Adams, began to experience persistent health problems which made it difficult for her to consistently perform her administrative duties at the high level to which she was accustomed. During her absence in the latter part of 1970, Mobley served as acting chairperson. In 1971, Adams resigned her position as chairperson and professor at FAMU and later assumed a leadership role in business at St. Augustine College in Raleigh, North Carolina. Because Mobley had demonstrated her ability as an effective classroom teacher, scholar, and professor who could serve as a skilled liaison with corporate leaders, Dr. Leedell W. Neyland, then Dean of the College of Arts and Sciences, recommended her immediate appointment as chairperson of the Department of Business. Upon accepting the appointment beginning 1971-72, she boldly proclaimed that she would make the business program at FAMU "the best in the United States." During her 32 years as chairperson of the Department of Business and Economics and Dean of the School of Business and Industry, she worked incessantly to achieve this lofty goal.

Mobley could not immediately take appropriate steps to initiate all of the changes in the department that she had visualized. Rather, she had to implement the traditional business curriculum and serve the student population which had been traditionally admitted. Courses leading to majors with the B.S. degree were accounting, general business administration, business education, secretarial science, and office management. From the very beginning, Mobley believed that business education, secretarial science, and office management should be housed in the College of Education; however the structure of the University required that these programs remain in the business department.

During the 1969-1970 academic year, the University adopted the *1969 Role and Scope Report* which essentially committed FAMU to becoming an "open door" university, catering to disadvantaged or culturally deprived students. President Perry led his faculty in adopting the land grant slogan, "Give Every Youth a Chance," and in articulating programs for working with victimized and deprived people; providing "restorative programs" for the weak; creating research models for training teachers for the disadvantaged; engaging in research concerning those individuals who are economically, socially, or ethically deprived; and training at the bachelor's level industrial technologists, who are above craftsmen but below professional engineers. Although a component of the *Role and Scope Report* emphasized that FAMU must provide the necessary resources to offer high-quality, relevant, competitive academic programs to our high-achieving, academically capable students, people throughout the state began to view FAMU as an institution for low-achieving, disadvantaged, culturally deprived students. In the Board of Regents State University System Master Plan, this view of FAMU prevailed.

While Mobley worked effectively within the requirements of the University's *Role and Scope*, she also continued to build on the momentum that she began in the mid-1960s recruiting high achieving, academically capable students for the discipline of accounting. By 1973, her recruiting of National Merit Achievement Scholars had gone nationwide, and the FAMU business program was bringing together one of the largest pools of potential black leaders in America. The recruiting process for accounting and other business programs will be discussed in detail in the next chapter.

In 1972, Neyland, still dean of the College of Arts and Sciences, combined the Department of Business with the Department of Economics, creating the Department of Business and Economics. Although the executive committee of the College opposed the combination, under Mobley's leadership it proved to be a productive and beneficial union for both business and economics. Further, this union was an important transition toward the creation of SBI two years later.

In October, 1973 when it became evident that a reorganization of the University would establish a separate school for business and economics, Mobley and her staff presented a comprehensive proposal for the new school. In addition to its traditional programs in business and economics, the new proposal called for (1) an institute for Advanced Study in Business Management; (2) a Human Resources Management Center; (3) Business Education for Developing Communities and Countries; (4) a Master of Business Administration Program; *(5)* flexible mini-courses with computer assisted teaching technologies and techniques. Also, the proposal called for a two-week business summer camp for eleventh grade students under the assumption that this deliberate and dramatic action would redirect students from the more established programs toward new opportunities in Corporate America. Her estimated cost for these projects reached $560,000. Although she did not receive the authority or the resources to fully implement the programs requested in the proposal, many of the ideas were implemented later, and her call for a program in Human Resources Management (traditionally Industrial Relations) was initiated in 1974. The proposal for summer camps was also implemented.

The Board of Regents (BOR) did not approve SBI's request for a Master of Business Administration (M.B.A.) program at that time; however, on April 7, 1975 it authorized the establishment of a Center for Human Resources Management in the new business school and designated it as one of 23 programs of distinction in the statewide master plan. The Center for Human Resources Management began under the direction of Shirley Burggraf, Ph.D., Case Western Reserve and chair of the Division of Economics and Development, who was assisted by Willie Bailey, Ph.D., University of Illinois. The purpose of the program was to train people for jobs in labor relations, personnel management, as affirmative action officers, as expert witnesses, and to provide in service- training for those in Public Sector Bargaining in Florida as well as other local and state employees. With the approval of this center, FAMU could boast of having the most prestigious labor program in the state, and of being the only historically black college or university in the United States with such a program.

Dean Mobley stated in the *SBI Report* (June 1975) that the program in Human Resources management was timely because "The passage of Florida's Public Sector Bargaining law and the growth of unionization in the South have created an increased regional concern with the problems of Industrial Relations and Personnel Management." She insisted that "Proliferating new programs such as Affirmative Action, Public Sector Bargaining, and the Occupational Safety Health Act (OSHA) have created a burgeoning need for new types of trained mediators, arbitrators, expert witnesses, industrial hygienists, investigators, affirmative action officers, etc., for the resolution of industrial, public, and community disputes."

Less than one year after the approval of the Center, dissatisfaction among university faculty members in Florida over meager salary raises from 1972 to 1974 led to an affirmative vote on March 2-3, 1976 for collective bargaining throughout the State University System. At that time, courses were already available in SBI, and an outstanding cadre of adjunct professors who were experts in their' various fields had been secured to assist the small permanent faculty. The adjuncts for the Center included such outstanding persons as: Charlie Freeman, Chairman of the Public Employees Relations Commission; Carl B. Lange, III, Director of Governmental Relations, Florida Education Association; Jess McCrary, Industrial Relations Commission Judge; Curtis Mack, Director of the Professional Employees Relations Commission; Wilkie Ferguson, Industrial Claims Court Judge; and others. Subsequently, in the fall of 1976, Mobley and her staff recruited Addis Taylor, who later received his Ph.D. from Florida State University. He was a member of the

American Board of Arbitration who had outstanding experiences in industrial and labor relations. He was subsequently appointed as the Director of the Center for Human Resources Management. He was joined that year by George R. Auzenne, M.Ed., Michigan State University, who had served as executive director of the Florida Teacher Association for approximately three years.

In addition to well selected course offerings, the Center held seminars and workshops on and off campus, and provided in-service assistance to state and local agencies. Upon satisfactorily completing five courses in the Center, one would be awarded a certificate in (Labor Relations) Human Resources; and upon completing eight courses one would be awarded an advanced certificate. Over the years, the Center for Human Resources Management made many significant contributions to various agencies in the state of Florida. During the reorganization of the University in 1982-1983, the Center was transferred to the College of Arts and Sciences where it functioned as a meaningful educational unit of the University.

In January of 1974, FAMU began implementing its reorganized structure which was developed after a year-long study by a select committee of 40 professors and administrators. According to Dr. Gertrude L. Simmonds, then Vice President for Academic Affairs, the reorganization was designed to break up "isolated academic empires." Later in the 1975-1976 *FAMU Bulletin* it was stated: "In response to the changing occupational needs and interests of students and in an effort to attract a more diversified student population to the University, FAMU has undergone a reorganization." As a result, the University had three colleges and four schools: the College of Education; the College of Humanities and Social Sciences; the College of Science and Technology; the School Architecture; the School of Nursing; the School of Pharmacy; and the School of Business and Industry. The new SBI announced four divisions - Control and Financial Services; Business Education, Secretarial Science and Office Management; Management Sciences and Economic Development. This organization structure lasted from January to August, 1974.

Almost sixty years after the first formal curriculum was established in business and commerce, the changing programs in business and business related courses had evolved into an autonomous unit—a unique School of Business and Industry. In keeping with Mobley's request, in the fall of 1974, business education, secretarial science and office management were transferred to the College of Education in the reorganization. Mobley was left with business and economics courses and given a mandate by President Perry to build the strong business school of which she had dreamed. According to the *General University Catalog*, 1975-1976, SBI had three divisions: Management Sciences, Control and Financial Services, and Economics and Development. Within those divisions students could earn the B.S. degree in the areas of marketing, management, general business administration, accounting and finance and the B.A. or B.S. in Economics. Her ambitious plan for recruiting high achieving students could not be fully implemented in 1975-1976 for all business programs because many students who had been admitted under the general admissions regulations were already in the academic pipeline. The majority of the students enrolled in SBI were not the high-achievers that Mobley expected in the new school; therefore, she began her fight to have SBI designated as a limited access school where higher standards could be required.

So as Mobley sought to lead her faculty into effectively serving students admitted under the University's general requirements, she intensified her effort to implement changes that she had visualized. These included continuously raising admission standards; creating an innovative curriculum; increasing academic rigor; providing professional development training for students; effecting meaningful internship programs; and establishing effective partnerships with the corporate world. Utilizing an unconventional curriculum for the "total development of business students," Mobley began pursuit of her self-imposed challenge to make SBI "the best in the United States."

3 ESTABLISHING A NON-TRADITIONAL BUSINESS SCHOOL

In January of 1974, Dean Sybil C. Mobley and her relatively small faculty and staff began the highly intricate and challenging task of establishing a unique, innovative business school. They were determined that they would not mimic large, successful business schools like Harvard, Stanford, and Wharton, but would design a school with creative and supportive training environments that would ensure the full development of students academically, professionally, and socially. Mobley and her faculty and staff realized that the demands of the business world would require preparation that went far beyond mere technical competence. They fully realized that graduates joining Corporate America must have technical competence, sound communication skills, business sophistication, social skills, and strong personal leadership qualities. Thus, they set out on uncharted waters to design and implement academic and professional programs which would send "totally developed business graduates" into the business community.

Even the name of the School of Business and Industry (SBI) was a break with tradition, for it was perhaps the first business school in the nation to use this nomenclature. To Mobley, the name had real meaning. In a moving address to her faculty and students in January 1974, she stressed the unique characteristics of the school. She further emphasized that while the new school would include the traditional concerns of most business schools with management, accounting, and finance programs that are described by the term "business," the word "industry" describes inherent concerns for economic development. She assured her audience that when SBI assumed this new name, it was "looking around the corner to get the jump on the others." She predicted that business schools of the future would become increasingly concerned with industrial and economic development, and SBI would already be setting the pace. Her words were somewhat prophetic, for an increasingly large number of business programs have adopted this name.

From its early beginnings, SBI endeavored to take approaches to business education which in many ways set the standards for other schools. All the while, Mobley and her faculty and staff immediately began to implement her ideas in academic reform and professional development. For approximately six years she was somewhat hampered by the University's liberal admission requirements. As late as 1980, FAMU's *General Catalog* stated that "admission to the School of Business and Industry is directed to the admission requirements of the University as stated elsewhere in the catalog." For example, an in-state graduate of an accredited high school was required to have a "C" or better in academic subjects and a minimum score of 200 on the Florida State-Wide Twelfth Grade Test (equivalent to 650 on the SAT).

Mobley realized that she could not build quality business programs using minimum university admission requirements. Since her new approaches to business training were predicated on a "very special faculty" and high-achieving students whom she called "Superstars," for a few years she was forced to run virtually a dual program—one for Superstars and another for students admitted under minimum requirements. However, in the field of accounting, Mobley began requesting rigorous admission standards as early as 1969, despite the University's near open door admission policy. Using her contacts with "Big Eight" CPA firms, General Electric, IBM, and with several other industrial companies she was able to find increasing funding for the recruitment program that she visualized. In her article in the Autumn 1970, edition of the *Waterhouse Review*, Mobley stated: "last year, one major accounting firm sponsored a recruitment banquet at a major hotel in Miami for top seniors from the city's twenty-one high schools. The results were so impressive that the firm has agreed to sponsor a similar banquet next year-not just in Miami but in other major cities as well." Over the next few years this form of recruiting expanded rapidly.

For example, on March 11, 1973, she encouraged fourteen of the nation's leading firms to sponsor the first banquet in the Chicago area for National Merit Achievement Scholarship Semifinalists at the Palmer House in Chicago, Illinois. Seventy-six young Superstars attended that banquet, and many chose to matriculate at FAMU in the fall of 1973. At that time SBI required freshmen entering accounting to have a minimum score of 950 on the SAT and 20 on the ACT. By the beginning of the 1980s, SBI began requiring admission scores of 1,000 on the SAT or 23 on the ACT. Admission scores for all programs in SBI progressively increased in the 1980s. The University finally acceded to Mobley's insistence that SBI must establish and maintain higher admission standards than most other colleges and schools. The 1981-1982 *General Catalog* stipulated that SBI's "Requirements include all University Admission requirements as well as those listed for the School of Business and Industry in the Special Admission section of the catalog." Also, in 1981-1982 the Board of Regents and the University recognized SBI as a limited access school which was at liberty to set higher and more rigorous standards. Thus, Mobley and her staff began to implement academic changes—more thoroughly vet potential students, demand higher admission scores, improve the Leadership Program (Professional Development) with intensified training in professional development, and expand the internship process. The increased standards and rigor of SBI programs rapidly eliminated students who had been admitted under minimum University requirements, and discouraged low-achieving students from seeking admission to SBI.

From 1974 to 1981, SBI offered the Bachelor of Science degree in the following areas: marketing, management, general business administration, accounting, finance, and economics.

In the fall of 1982, the Division of Economics and Development, was transferred to the College of Arts and Sciences and stayed there until well after Dr. Mobley's retirement. In 2011 subsequent to the retirement of the long-term chair, Shirley Burggraf—widely considered to be the cause of the original rift—University reorganization reunited the Department of Economics with SBI.

However, at the time in 1982, the transfer of the Division of Economics and Development left SBI with just two divisions: Control and Financial Services and Management Sciences. The division of Control and Financial Services alternated its chairmanship from 1974 and 1982 between Professor James Bryant and Dr. Forrest Thompson. The Division of Management Sciences changed chairmen often during the 1970s and early 1980s with those serving included Dr. Andrew Honeycutt, Dr. Norman Ware, Dr. Charles R. Russell, Dr. Wayne Perry, and Dr. Robert Atkinson. In the mid 1980s and 1990s SBI had a very flat administrative structure of two divisions—Academic Programs and Professional Development. The Division of Academic Programs was under the directorship of Dr. Sid Credle, who now serves as the Dean of the School of Business at Hampton University; and later Dr. Richard Wilson who remains in service to SBI as an associate professor and the current Chair of the newly reinstated department of Economics and Professional Leadership Development. Throughout Dr. Mobley's tenure as dean, Professional Development was headed by several faculty members and administrators including Dr. George Clark, Thomas Jefferson, Booker Daniels, and Dr. Abigail Thompkins. However, Dr. Amos Bradford who retired as an associate professor at the end of the 2012-2013 academic year was the long-standing chair of the Professional Development program.

Within the new organizational structure of the early 1980s, instead of six distinct majors, SBI now offered the B.S. in accounting and in business administration. The organizational structure was consistent throughout the 1980's and early 1990's. As early as 1978, the BOR approved a traditional one-year Master of Business Administration (M.B.A.). While the traditional M.B.A. remained intact, major emphasis in SBI started to take focus on a five-year Professional M.B.A. program which was implemented in 1994-1995. The two division directors reported directly to Dean Mobley. The divisions were supported by a well-developed internship office under Mrs. Faye Williams and later Ms. Doris Corbett, now retired, which emphasized behavioral competence and business sophistication; and an office of recruitment, under Mr. O'Hara Hannah, which worked incessantly to find and annually attract a group of high- achieving Superstars from high schools across the nation.

How do you convince a very confident, very smart, much sought after student to come to rural Tallahassee Florida instead of Harvard or Brown University? Recruiting a Superstar was no easy task. In the 1980's blacks gained unprecedented access to higher education in the United States. Unlike earlier eras when segregation and unfavorable admission policies at majority institutions virtually guaranteed a cadre of talented black students would attend HBCUs, Mobley had a consistent fight with schools like Harvard University to recruit black National Merit/Achievement Scholars and Scholarship Finalists. National Merit and National Achievement Scholars and Finalists make up roughly 3% of graduating high school students and are chosen on the basis of qualifying test scores on the Preliminary Scholastic Achievement Test/National Merit Scholarship Qualifying Test (PSAT/NMSQT) and an application packet.

Due to the relative low numbers of black students recognized by the National Merit Scholarship Corporation, Dean Mobley was determined to recruit as many as possible. She could be found in her office many late nights, personally signing "Dear Superstar" letters, calling the homes of high-performing students, speaking with them and their parents, extolling the virtues of the SBI program. A May 17, 1987 article *St. Petersburg Times*, "Students see their future at FAMU" chronicled then SBI Senior Roy Washington's initial telephone conversation with Dean Mobley when she personally called him at his parents' home as a high school senior. The conversation started with "Hello, superstar, my name is Sybil Mobley, Dean of the School of Business and Industry. Do you know you're a superstar?" Many Superstars found the undeniable appeal in that simple statement.

In one instance, Dr. Mobley's In fact, an article in the February 1, 2001 issue of *Black Issues in Higher Education* entitled "FAMU ties Harvard in Recruitment of National Achievement Scholars" stated that "Since 1988, FAMU has been among the nation's top five recruiters of National Achievement Scholars." Notwithstanding that current year's tie between FAMU and Harvard, the article goes on to expound on FAMU's success in recruiting National Merit Scholars, "FAMU earned the top spot in academia for three years—1992, 1995 and 1997."

Through a three-pronged attack, 1) the recruitment of nationally recognized black youth, 2) the awarding of both "4-year" and "renewable" scholarships in various amounts, 3), the promise of highly-paid internships, and later permanent placement salaries, Mobley brought academic content, business savvy, and leadership acumen to a formidable base of the nation's best and brightest black business students throughout the 1970's, 1980's, 1990's; well beyond retirement in 2003.

In addition to Mobley's unprecedented success in recruiting the nation's top black students, she knew that in order to ensure the academic and professional success of those bright students, a top-notch faculty was necessary. To ensure the effective implementation of the programs she envisioned it was essential for Mobley to assemble a faculty which would internalize her overall goals and objectives. Thus, in recruiting faculty members for SBI's academic programs she set the major requirements as an "earned doctorate, sharp mind, and a commitment to both excellence in teaching and research of impact." In seeking this "very special faculty," she would frequently ask these questions in her advertisements: "Do you view your doctorate as having landed you at take-off position? Are you ready, willing, and able to grow both personally and professionally? Are you willing to submit yourself to a period of developing any missing competencies and gaining rich experiences and exposures?" Mobley would then outline the types of competencies and experiences that SBI faculty needed such as: computer sophistication, in-depth global perspective, foreign language competencies, overseas experience, memory skills, speed reading, rich business experience, and personal, interpersonal and organizational skills.

Always emphasizing the unique and highly innovative approaches of SBI to academic and professional training, Mobley insisted on asking candidates for faculty positions if they could come with a "clean sheet" to explore new approaches, new frontiers, and new standards of excellence. She further advised prospective professors that they must be able to seek new teaching methodologies, engage in team teaching, and do research for impact in business. She generally concluded her advertisement materials with: "Can you think big? Do you have a positive self-image? Can you envision yourself as a leader, a pace-setter, and a major player in the global academic community?" She would advise candidates that if they could answer "yes" to the above questions and concerns, they should apply and learn if they qualified for a career of the future that provides growth, accomplishment, self-actualization, and lucrative rewards.

In her efforts to establish a "very special faculty," Mobley focused her attention on recruiting black doctorates, beginning with her graduate alma mater. During the 1970s, the SBI faculty included the following Ph. D.s from the University of Illinois: Willie Bailey, Charlie Carter, George Clark, Thomas W. Mason, Forrest Thompson and of course, Sybil C. Mobley. Other doctorates on the regular SBI faculty during this period were: Shirley Burggraf, Ph. D., Case Western Reserve; Jean-Marie Bannatte, Ph. D., University of Missouri; Larry A. Frieder, Ph. D., University of Arizona; Andrew Honeycutt, Ph. D., Harvard University; I. Eugene McNeill, Ph. D. University of Texas; Delores M. Robinson, Ph. D., University of Wisconsin; Charles R. Russell, Ph. D., Florida State University, and Gloria Rislov, Ph. D., Wayne State University. Frequently, Mobley would bring in visiting faculty from industry, many of whom also held the doctorate.

When one considers the difficulty of attracting doctorates to a young beginning school, the persuasive power of Mobley can be clearly discerned. Faculty members who were recruited without the Ph. D. were advised that they must complete it within a stipulated period of time if they expected continuous employment. Thus many who joined the SBI faculty without the earned doctorate subsequently completed their programs. Further, Mobley encouraged her accounting faculty to seek to become Certified Public Accountants (CPA). In 1976, a total of seven faculty members, including Dean Mobley, in the Division of Control and Financial Services had become CPAs. By any measure, Mobley assembled a well-trained, competent faculty who dedicated themselves to the SBI Leadership Program which employed the interactive method. Even though the conditions were far from being ideal, together they designed and developed a new school with a new philosophy of business education which began to attract attention throughout America.

Recognizing that America's colleges and universities were not graduating enough African American doctorates in business to provide well-qualified professors for the classroom, Mobley devised a plan to help SBI produce its own. She approached various accounting firms and requested support for faculty fellowship grants for doctoral study, doctoral research grants, and scholarship funds. Arthur Andersen Foundation of Chicago, Illinois was the first company to provide funds for the specific support of doctoral study. In a letter to

Dean Mobley dated January *25,* 1973 from Claude Rogers, Representing the Foundation, he stated:

> This is a $20,000 grant to provide funds for Professor Benjamin Newhouse, or other accounting professors designated by you, to pursue Doctoral Studies. You indicated that it would take approximately two years of concentrated study for Professor Newhouse to complete his studies and a major portion of his dissertation. We will provide a grant of $10,000 annually for two years for this purpose.

In addition to the grant for doctoral studies, the Foundation provided at the same time, a doctoral research grant of $5,000 for one year to assist a new faculty member in completing the research for the dissertation.

Subsequent to the grants by Arthur Andersen and Co. Foundation, other firms assisted in faculty development by providing direct grants for faculty development, by providing specialists as visiting faculty in areas of need, and by supporting faculty who had completed all but the dissertation (A.B.D.). The corporate world was invaluable to Mobley in her early efforts to establish a quality faculty.

The School of Business and Industry began its early years housed in extremely poor, overcrowded facilities on the third and fourth floors of Tucker Hall. Shortly after the 1974-1975 academic year began, the central administration announced that Tucker Hall would be renovated during the spring and that all academic units would be transferred to temporary locations. Mobley assured her faculty and staff in a memorandum dated January 14, 1975, that "this inconvenience would bear dividends in the future because the entire campus is going to be converted into one of the most beautiful campuses anywhere." In the meantime, SBI faculty and staff offices were relocated to the Perry Paige Building: the first floor lobby housed the SBI Library, and the second floor lobby was made into offices for the Dean, assistant Dean and secretarial offices. Because most of the offices were petitioned stalls, it became known as the "cow pasture." SBI experienced severe "growing pains" due to the campus-wide renovation. However, Mobley placed a positive spin on the temporary discomforts and encouraged the faculty and staff to develop "closer bonds than ever." She assured them that SBI would soon have "a new, beautiful, modern, specifically designed building to itself."

While waiting for the new building, Mobley and her faculty were again transferred to Lee Hall, which had recently been vacated by the central administration which was relocated to the newly renovated Foote-Hilyer Administration Center (Old Hospital). Mobley was assigned the office formerly occupied by President B. L. Perry. The fact that some of her faculty were spread out in other facilities did not deter her from encouraging faculty solidarity as she forged ahead to build a unique, innovative business school. Despite her good intentions, Mobley's aggressive pursuit of support and her insistence that the *Role and Scope* of FAMU was inadequate to accommodate her vision for business programs brought her into conflict with central administration on multiple occasions.

In the midst of these difficult times for SBI, Mobley became temporarily disenchanted with restrictions that were placed on her in seeking support for her school, and the negative responses of the FAMU central administration to her creative and progressive ideas. In October 1974, nine months after she took over the deanship, she submitted her resignation to vice president for academic affairs, Dr. Gertrude L. Simmons and President B. L. Perry. Appearing before her faculty on October 18, 1974, she advised them that the president had accepted her recommendation that Andrew Honeycutt be named Interim Dean. After a brief national search for a new dean, they did not find anyone of Mobley's caliber, and the search was called off. Rumors abounded that Mobley and her faculty would take their innovative business program to another unnamed university, though this plan was never publicly stated. However, at the administrative level, cooler heads soon began to prevail, and the president and vice president for academic affairs persuaded Mobley to resume her position as dean of SBI. Thus, the business programs moved forward without any noticeable disruptions.

It was in early 1982 that the actual work began on what is now called the "South Wing" of the SBI building. Using the academic and professional programs that Mobley and her faculty and staff had conceptualized, the building was designed by Clemons and Rutherford and a black architect, Don Stuhi Associates of Cambridge, Massachusetts. The new five-floor building, which has

49,260 general square footage, was built at a cost of $4,904.030 and was occupied in August 1983.

A booklet describing the new building was entitled *The Building that Says Business*. It was boldly announced that the building "will house the nationally recognized SBI Leadership Program and will stand as a tribute to the world of business and industry." Special features of the building included a state of the art fully equipped computer center, two United Nations-type classrooms, team and meeting rooms, seminar rooms, business library facilities, shower and dressing facilities, and student and faculty lounges. This design enabled the faculty and staff to more effectively implement the SBI sanctuary approach. Under this specific methodology, "students were to be immersed in a business culture which assured that they would think and talk business all day, every day." The overriding belief of Mobley and her faculty and staff was that the unique features of the building would "guarantee a business environment which will not only be conducive to learning, but will also facilitate adjustment to the business world."

The Sybil C. Mobley School of Business and Industry, so named in 2008, was originally designated the S131 building. Upon approaching the entrance to S131, in an external area the SBI students fondly call the SBI Set, one cannot miss one major manifestation of Dean Mobley's genius—"a wall extending two floors artfully displays the logos of some of the nation's leading businesses on SBI's "Big Board." The Big Board name was adopted from the nickname of the New York Stock Exchange. In the early 1980s, Mobley conceived the idea of establishing the SBI Big Board to enhance the business environment of the school and to feature those businesses that made major commitments to the endowment of scholarships at the school. Each company that gave $100,000 or more to the school was to be recognized with a bronze logo on the Big Board. Because the State of Florida would match endowment grants at a fifty percent rate, almost immediately, many companies accepted the invitation to secure their places on the SBI Big Board. *Newsweek* pointed out in a May 24, 1982 issue that "twenty companies agreed to donate $100,000 each toward building an endowment fund..." This magnificent response came more than a year before the new SBI building was actually occupied.

According to the *SBI Minutes* of January 17, 1984, Roger Smith, Chairman of the Board of General Motors, actually presented the first logo to be placed on the SBI Big Board. He boldly stated: "I can't think of a finer place to display the GM logo." Further, Smith was quoted in the February 2, 1984 issue of the *Daytona Times* as saying: "The reasons for our support are obvious: We are impressed with what you have done; we have confidence in what you will do. But the success of Dr. Mobley and SBI is more than just impressive—it is rare... This is not a contribution; it is an investment in you." This was indeed a memorable occasion for it brought the major media networks (ABC, CBS, and NBC) to the campus. Subsequently, some of the early firms to join General Motors on The SBI Big Board were Anheuser-Busch Companies, General Electric Foundation, Arthur Andersen & Co., Honeywell, Alcoa, Hershey, Champion International, Corning, Owens-Illinois, Atlantic Richfield Foundation, Southeast Bank, Emerson, CIGNA, DuPont, Pizza Hut, American Brands Inc., and Ernst & Whitney.

Nearly fourteen years later, the *Tallahassee Democrat* (February 25, 1996) reported that more than 70 Fortune 500 companies had donated $100,000 or more to SBI's scholarship endowment fund. Although only large corporations had been encouraged to secure places on the Big Board, there has been one notable exception. On February 23, 1996, SBI alumni called "The SBI Force" presented SBI with their gift of $ 100,000 to claim a space on the SBI Big Board. Mobley proclaimed that this was "probably the biggest day I've experienced here."

Although Mobley aggressively sought contributions from businesses and individuals she insisted that "participation in the SBI Big Board is not for sale." Rather she reminded her public that:

> It is reserved for those firms with whom we have mutual commitment to the betterment of society, by the joint production of competent people and competitive products. The big board is big because of the greatness of the firms represented on it; because of the concept of joint corporate and academic effort; because of the perpetuity that it assures with endowment funds; and because of the opportunity provided for deserving youth throughout that perpetuity.

Prior to Mobley's retirement, all original spaces on the Big Board were filled, representing $15 million generated for the school. Though expanded several times, space and other constraints preclude the possibility of further expanding the Big Board. However, Mobley was known to have forwarded several additional development plans prior to her retirement. She was quoted as saying that these additional projects, when implemented would eventually dwarf the results of the phenomenally successful SBI Big Board.

The SBI Big Board is not only a source of funding for scholarship and endowments, but it is a listing of the school's major corporate partners who jointly committed to help ensure the high standards of excellence through the programs that SBI established. Many members of The SBI Force can fondly point out various the companies at which they held internships, at which they accepted permanent positions, companies that funded their scholarships, and firms at which they are currently employed and enjoy satisfying and lucrative careers.

Upon entering the SBI building which says "Business," one was immediately imbued with a sense of business culture. On weekdays, dark business suit-clad students populated the classrooms, team rooms, and halls on the five floors of the building until late each night. Each floor is named for an international business/center of commerce. Each floor also contains an original mural bearing the likeness of the centers of commerce at that time. The ground floor represented Wall Street, New York, United States, and included a working ticker-tape outside the Bull and Bear Lounge. The first floor houses a colorful mural, showing business as usual at the time on Harambee Avenue, in Nairobi Kenya's Central Business District. The first floor also housed the SBI Library, the dean's office and other administrative offices. The second floor was Des Voix Road, Hong Kong. The third floor represented Avenida Paulista in Sao Paulo Brazil's Paulista Financial Center. Lastly, the fourth floor hall is Threadneedle Street which in London, U.K is the home of the Bank of England. In SBI, the fourth floor housed the very plush, state of the art, and very "corporate" SBI Boardroom. Additionally, corporate donations made possible the completion of separate graduate and undergraduate PC computer labs—revolutionary at the time. Subsequently, the entering classes for the remainder of the 1980s garnered a bit of pride from the "state of the art" business building and the perceived uniqueness of the setting, thus further enhancing the "sanctuary environment" within the walls of SBI.

In December 1994, SBI celebrated the expansion of its building facilities with the opening of the newly constructed, specially designed east wing. This new wing, which consisted of four stories and 30,000 square feet, was designed by Gilchrist and Crowe Architects and built by the Ajax construction Company, both of Tallahassee at a-total cost of $4,010,478. The east wing was designed to extend the SBI Sanctuary approach which began in the main building. The building consists primarily of business laboratories, team rooms, one classroom and faculty offices. It also housed a new computer laboratory and a sophisticated communication system that permitted teachers to monitor and communicate with students in the specially designed team rooms. Another special feature of the building was the scholars suite designed to accommodate eminent scholars, visiting corporate scholars, international scholars, and selected researchers in the field of business, though it now houses the

SBI Office of Student Services. With the construction of the east wing, fifty additional parking spaces were added to accommodate increased traffic in the SBI area.

With the east wing completed and occupied, the next step on the SBI Master Plan was construction of the west and north wings, which commenced in 1999. Completed in 2002, the four wings now encircle a courtyard area called the SBI Quadrangle. The SBI Quad has been home to many corporate-sponsored recruitment fairs and SBI open houses. Dr. Mobley's dream is that one day the courtyard will be a covered atrium that will become the SBI Global Culture Plaza. Her vision is for this plaza to one day serve as an effective laboratory as it is converted into one nation after another to accommodate the global thrust of the SBI curriculum. Mobley's long-range plan also included a state-of-the-art multi-level parking facility for SBI. The proposed building with multi-level parking facilities would be a state-of-the-art structure; however, the University has since built a multi-level parking structure nearby.

East Wing, School of Business and Industry

After the first building (the South Wing) was constructed, the State University System of Florida conducted program reviews of all SUS business administration programs (BOR. 84-86) in June 1984. The following excerpt from the review of SBI at FAMU was an enthusiastic endorsement of the new, non-traditional school:

> The program of the School of Business and Industry at Florida A&M University is not only different from other schools of business in Florida, but it is unique among schools of business in the nation. It is a jewel among schools of business and a national center of excellence...In terms of value added, SBI surely ranks with the best institutions in the country...the SBI program has been recognized by the consultants as unique and a recognized model for excellence.

For nearly two decades, the unique characteristics of SBI's "total development" methodology were virtually ignored by America's prestigious schools of business, but warmly embraced and supported by corporate America. However, as we moved toward the 21st century, the cadre of scholars that evaluated SBI saw it as a "national center of excellence" which ranked with the "best institutions in the country." Increasingly, schools of business began to realize that the leadership and professional development methods begun by SBI more than 35 years ago were indeed essential in preparing managers/leaders for the national and global marketplace.

Mobley's early ideas of business education based on a sound Leadership Program which included structured professional development and diversified internships appeared to be original and untried practices among American schools of business. A cursory examination of curricula throughout prestigious business schools of the time revealed that many adopted concepts in business education pioneered by Mobley and her faculty in the early 1970s. In fact, the May 16, 1991 issue of Business Week reported that:

> Wharton is embarking on an overhaul of its M.B.A. program. The aim: to turn out what Wharton hopes will be the business leaders, not just financiers, of the 21st century. The

makeover, said Wharton Dean, Thomas P. Gerrity, was "bold, dramatic, and revolutionary.

While the changes announced by Dean Gerrity may have been revolutionary for Wharton, the record shows that they were, in many ways, a replica of SBI's Leadership Program for business education which formally began in 1974. SBI's Leadership program has been well documented in FAMU's University catalogs and other publications, and had formed the undergirding philosophy of business training for baccalaureate and subsequent M.B.A. training at FAMU.

In an article by *Fortune* (July 20, 1991) it was stated that: "Major business schools including Wharton, Columbia, and Chicago have finally undertaken serious market research to determine what their customers want—and whether they are delivering it (short answer: no)." In the same article a Wharton representative boasted: "This is the first time that any curriculum is really responsive to market requirements." Accordingly, today, most prestigious business schools and many other professional schools (i.e. architecture, journalism, and pharmacy) at major universities in the United States have formalized programs in professional development and/or "soft skills."

Although it may have been the "first time that any curriculum" at those schools had been responsive to market requirements, from the outset of Mobley's leadership as chairperson of the Department of Business, she insisted that the business program at FAMU be customer-oriented and market-driven. In addition to working in various businesses and governmental agencies for valuable learning experiences, she took an initial survey in 1971 to determine what the corporate community wanted. Surveys of corporate partners which provide internships and hire SBI graduates continue as a standard part of the program. Beginning with its inception in 1974, SBI formally sought the input of business executives in order to assure that its overall Leadership Program was customer-oriented and market-driven. In Lee Smith's article in *Fortune* (December 28, 1981) Mobley was lavishly praised for her ability to produce graduates at SBI with the technical and behavioral competencies that the corporate community desired. Smith quoted Mobley as saying:

We tell those in corporate America—if they can give us the specs of what they want—we can produce it. The buyers for the class of '81 included IBM (eight), Coopers & Lybrand (six), Continental Illinois (three), and Chase Manhattan (three).

Other publications of the era such as the *Tallahassee Democrat* (1978), *Newsweek* (May 24, 1982), and the *National Black Monitor* (March, 1981) published articles supporting SBI's early interactive training program with corporate America.

Beginning with a new philosophy of business education, with an outstanding cadre of well-trained professors, with high-achieving student Superstars, with a creative, innovative curriculum, and with an enviable internship and placement record in the corporate world, Mobley, her faculty and staff demonstrated to the world the true merits of SBI—a non-traditional business school.

4 DEVELOPING THE SBI LEADERSHIP PROGRAM

In an effort to send forth to corporate America a cadre of "totally developed business graduates," it was essential for SBI to develop from its very beginning a unique Leadership Program to encompass the academic, professional and practical aspects of business education. The Leadership Program was conceived in 1974 as one of total development. Its primary objective was to prepare students to assume professional positions in the management of organizations of varying sizes and diverse technologies. Within the total development system, the Leadership Program was designed to assure well-rounded graduates capable of high level performance in the complex, dynamic world of business. All programs and activities in SBI were directed toward accomplishing established objectives through the development of both technical competence and positive personal qualities. The focus of the total development system was the development of competencies which transcended academic disciplines and was increasingly based on a global perspective as the arena of analysis.

Mobley and her faculty recognized that technical competence could best be achieved through an academic program characterized by an interdisciplinary approach that provided students with (1) a liberal education which included well-selected courses in the areas of communications, mathematics, natural sciences, behavioral and social sciences, and humanities and fine arts; (2) an understanding of how a global market economy works and how businesses and individuals relate to and are influenced by the world's economic systems; and (3) academic preparation in specialized areas of business and economics. Positive personal qualities were to be developed through a series of required diversified leadership experiences primarily in the Division of Professional Development which were scheduled throughout the curriculum of a student's college career. Although these experiences were tailored to address each student's strengths and weaknesses, they generally included extensive extra-class readings, team activities, leadership roles, self-analysis, and career planning.

According to Mobley and her faculty in documents published in the late 1970s, the SBI Leadership Program employed the interactive method. This relied on extensive use of teams and corporation-based simulations which exposed students to the introductory, intermediate, and advanced levels of business concepts in assigned roles of entry-level, middle-level, and top-level management. The mastery of course content offered under the Division of Academic Programs was not viewed as an end in itself. Rather, it was seen as a currently relevant instrument for the development of strong personal qualities such as assertiveness, decisiveness, integrity, discipline, analytic problem-solving skills, resourcefulness, results orientation, business sophistication, and communication and leadership skills. The Interactive Methodology articulated and interposed the three major components of the Leadership Program—the academic program, professional development, and the internship process.

The SBI process was cumulative; therefore, it was impossible to dichotomize academic programs and professional development of students into distinct components. In the application of SBI's interactive methodology, each component was dependent upon the other. Almost from the very beginning, the SBI process was described by Mobley and her faculty as follows:

> At each level, the focus is on the acquisition of specific behavioral competencies and a body of academic content that is applied at each subsequent level. However, application of competencies acquired at each level must be applied at all subsequent levels of both Professional Development (PD) and academic courses. Likewise, the academic knowledge acquired at each level must be applied at all subsequent levels of both PD and Academic courses. At each level, both behavioral

competencies and academic content constitute prerequisites for subsequent levels. Both academic and PD courses constitute application labs for behavioral competencies and academic content. Students must be evaluated in each academic course on both the mastery of the content and the application of the competencies required at that level; students must be evaluated at each PD level on both the mastery of the content and the application of competencies required at that level. Therefore, PD and academic courses constitute constant quality control checks for each other. However, school-wide quality controls are needed to serve as "effectiveness" master controls. These controls will be in the form of SBI exams and designated performances.

The programmatic effect of this strategy is that students must be graded in both PD and academic courses on the cumulative internalization of prior development. To be operative, the quality controls must be simple, relevant, and standardized. For example, although dependability is the specific focus at the freshman level, it must be evaluated at all levels (both PD and academic) by recording behavior such as promptness and consistency in class attendance, class assignments, and appointments.

The most essential aspect of the interactive method was that a competitive atmosphere was created which honed the skills of students to razor-sharp efficiency. The end product of this experience was a poised, mature, competitive young business person, capable of embracing new and emerging business concepts, and eager to take on the responsibilities of the business profession and to face the business world with confidence.

The records of SBI show that the Leadership Program has not been static, but an ever-changing concept designed to develop and enhance in business students the competencies and characteristics generally recognized to be essential for success. *The Leadership Manual for SBI 1978-1979* indicated that graduates should possess the following qualities:

Intellectual Ability	Integrity
Critical Thinking Skills	Openness
Analytical Ability	Commitment
Energy	Sense of Humor
Maturity	Enthusiasm
Perseverance	Creativity
Tough-Mindedness	

Although it was recognized initially that students would realize these qualities in varying degrees, under Sybil Mobley, SBI was uncompromising in requiring that all business students be exposed to and participate in the activities of the Leadership Program. The SBI curriculum was competency-based as opposed to content based, because competencies transcend content and outline its relevance.

The conceptual framework of the Leadership Program was predicated on three basic tenets: (1) Total Development, (2) The Sanctuary Approach, and (3) A Program for Students with Demonstrated Intellectual Ability. A brief explanation will be given for each of the tenets.

Total Development—One of the often repeated guiding principles of SBI is that it "is not sufficient to train for technical competency; it is necessary to also educate for responsibility and to maximize potential." Through the Leadership Program, SBI was consistently able to produce graduates capable of accepting the rigors and responsibilities of the world. Students prepared daily for the business world through a series of structured, confidence-building activities in the areas of oral communication, written communication, goal-setting, planning, and group dynamics. Participation and evaluation records were kept and included in the computation of the students' Leadership Quotient (LQ). This quotient was used as the basis for internships and for other selected practical activities related to business.

A Sanctuary Approach——this approach was designed to maintain close contact with the student from the initial recruiting activities until he or she completes the program. Through faculty and staff counseling, through interacting with other students, and through a series of planned activities, the student is provided opportunities to talk and think business all day, every day. The approach not only prevents student alienation, but it also brings students face to face with the realities of the world. According to the *Leadership Manual*, "the approach recognizes the predominately black composition of its student body and the predominately white face of the business world. Hence, a bicultural education is provided for both groups by bringing business and governmental leaders from throughout the country to the campus and through interaction with these professionals during internships." SBI students are placed in internships throughout the nation and the world. By offering group sessions with corporate executives and internship experiences as integral parts of the Leadership Program within the conceptual confines of a sanctuary, SBI was consistently able to produce students who were confident and competent to relate to a corporate environment at various levels of their collegiate education. The Sanctuary relates to the use of symbols, competitive team learning approaches, and in-house firms; therefore, students were literally immersed in a business setting where they internalized the business culture.

A Program for Students with Demonstrated Intellectual Ability—SBI also recognized that the changing nature of the business enterprise on the national and international levels demands employees who are technically competent and professionally versatile. With this in mind, SBI designed a rigorous, fast-paced program for students who had taken nationally competitive examinations while in high school, and had demonstrated superior academic and intellectual abilities.

In SBI's view, these high-ability students not only had the greatest chance for success in the business world, but represented the "product" now demanded by business leaders. Admission requirements for SBI were set at 1000 on the SAT or 23 on the ACT with a minimum "B" average in English and Mathematics. Increasingly, SBI began offering scholarships to students from the list of commended, semifinalists, and finalists of the National Achievement Scholarship Program and therefore was able to get students from the top five percent of high school graduates in the nation. This high selectivity factor resulted in a more homogeneous body of students based on intellectual achievement who were better able to withstand the pace and rigors of the program. Between 1995 and 1996 students were required to have a minimum score of 1050 on the SAT or 24 on the ACT, an impressive high school record, and three positive personal references. Because of increasing demand, the Fall 1997 requirements were increased to 1100 and 25 for the SAT and ACT respectively. In fact, in the article "At Florida A&M; Serious Business: in the October 7, 1997 issue of *The Washington Post*, Mobley almost bragged that competition was so "stiff" for the slots in the 1997 SBI freshman class, that SBI "virtually ceased to admit students with less than a 1200 on the SAT."

The foundation for achieving technical competence was gained through the Division of Academic Programs. With academic rigor established as a top priority of SBI, academic programs have experienced numerous changes over the years in efforts to prepare highly qualified graduates for the business world. During the late 1970s and 1980s, academic programs changed to incorporate just two baccalaureate programs—accounting and business administration. Dr. Wayne Perry was primarily responsible for the development of these programs and for laying the foundations for the first M.B.A. programs. Subsequently, the leadership of Academic Programs fell upon Dr. George Clark who served as interim director, and later upon Dr. Robert M. Atkinson, who worked with Dean Mobley in shifting the program's emphasis to the M.B.A. in the late 1980s. Upon the Dr. Atkinson's departure to corporate America, Dr. Vivian L. Carpenter served as director from 1993 to 1995; Dr. Sid H. Credle served from 1995 to 2000. Subsequently, Dr. Richard Wilson and Dr. Charles L. Evans also served in this capacity. Charles Evans also later served SBI as associate dean, and continued to at SBI until his death in 2013.

In preparing students for life and for the world of work, Mobley and her faculty and staff spoke frequently of the unique SBI process as the hallmark of the Leadership Program. SBI identified as its customers the students and the employers of students. The SBI process—the curriculum—was developed by considering the needs of customers and controls were established to assure the quality of the SBI Programs which delivered the process. Important features of the SBI process were: the SBI Methodology; high tech skills development; mini courses; fundamental concept courses; professional development; team teaching—integrated content and competitive team-based projects; internships; case studies; the unique physical facilities; and the unique student base, faculty, and administration.

The SBI curriculum recognized that in addition to sound academic preparation, students must be prepared to meet the "high-tech" challenge. However, the mastery of current technology alone was not adequate to function in a high-tech economy, for technology mastered in college may be obsolete by graduation. SBI's leadership thrust demanded that (in addition to requiring students to master current technology) it developed students who had expanded their capacity to learn efficiently through a series of enhanced learning skill courses (e.g. memory skills, speed reading, team management) followed by applications of the SBI Interactive Methodology. SBI graduates have expanded capacity as a result of having acquired the following competencies that transcend specific time-limited technologies: speed-reading, memory, flexibility, judgment, quality control, "triggered access," and high productivity. SBI operated on the assumption that both technical and non-technical competencies can be developed in an academic setting.

There was a common body of knowledge that every undergraduate student majoring in business was required to share. It comprised the following areas as stipulated in 1997 SBI publications:

(1)   A background in the concepts, processes, and institutions of the financing, production, marketing, and distribution functions of business enterprises;

(2)   A background in the economic and legal environment of business enterprises, along with consideration of the social and political influences on business;

(3)   A basic understanding of the concepts and methods;

(4)   A study of the theories of organizational behavior, interpersonal relationships, control and motivational systems; and

(5)   A study of administrative processes under conditions of uncertainty including integrating analysis and policy determination at the overall management level.

To assure that students were prepared for the challenges ahead, class attendance was compulsory in SBI; responsible professional conduct was required at all times; and students were required to earn a "C" or better in all required courses.

In order to challenge the undergraduate students academically and intellectually, SBI instituted a rigorous curriculum at both the lower and upper divisional levels. In addition to the considerably high scores on the SAT and ACT for undergraduate admission, students in the five-year M.B.A. program were expected to have a higher level of proficiency in mathematics. Students considering transferring from Florida's community colleges into the B.S. undergraduate program had to meet the standards set forth in the Florida State University System's mandated articulation agreement to be eligible for admission to SBI. Only first-time-in-college students were admitted to the Five-Year M.B.A. program.

All first-year undergraduate students were required to satisfy a common curriculum during the first two years:

Freshman Year	Semester Hours	Sophomore Year	Semester Hours
Financial Accounting	3	Managerial Accounting	3
Freshman Communication	3	Principles of Economics I & II	6
Statistics	3	Quantitative Methods I	3
Historical Survey I or II	3	Microcomputer Application	3
Introduction to Psychology	3	Electives	3
General Education Electives	6	World History	3
Science (electives)	6	General Education Electives	3
Total Hours	27		24

The traditional "general education" undergraduate model introduces college students to courses in their major fields at the Junior-year level. From the onset, Dean Mobley understood the importance of the SBI practice of immediately introducing freshman SBIans to business courses. Thus, taking the common core together within their first two years created a bond among very close cadres of

SBI's Superstars from their initial matriculation at FAMU and magnified the Sanctuary effect.

SBI Superstars bond and team-build at the
Annual FAMUSBI Club Overnight Initiation, Fall 1985

The third- and fourth-year students were offered a variety of well-chosen upper division courses which produced graduates who were academically, ethically, and professionally prepared to accept the challenges of current and future business organizations. So from time to time, the curriculum was upgraded to assure that students acquired the most current and relevant training possible.

In addition to the two baccalaureate programs and the five-year M.B.A., the one-year (three semester) M.B.A. degree has survived post-Mobley restructuring intact. It then required a minimum of 36 hours of graduate credit beyond the B.S. degree. The M.B.A. provided graduate education for individuals who wanted to pursue management careers in business and industry.

Through the intelligent use of electives, students were provided an opportunity to develop depth in one or more areas such as Accounting, Finance, Marketing, or Information Systems. The admission criteria for the one-year M.B.A. program included: (1) a baccalaureate degree from an accredited college or university; (2) a score of 600 or above on the General Management Admission Test

(GMAT); a minimum upper divisional GPA of 3.00; and (4) evidence of maturity and leadership. Persons accepted into the M.B.A. program were required to demonstrate fundamental competency in the areas of accounting, marketing, management, finance, economics, information systems analysis, quantitative methods, and professional skills.

Although the five-year professional Master of Business Administration (M.B.A.) was conceived and programmatically developed under Dr. Wayne Perry and Dr. Robert Atkinson, it was not officially approved by the Board of Regents (BOR) until August, 1995. Even before the BOR actually approved the program, SBI had sent out letters for the 1992-1993 academic year advising qualified students that they could enter the five-year program. Therefore, some students had already begun study in the five-year program prior to 1995. However, the five-year Master of Business Administration officially became SBI's flagship program in 1995 under the directorship of Dr. Sid Credle. As stated earlier, only first-time-in-college students were admitted to the five-year program. Because the program emphasized enhanced learning systems and specialized methodologies to accelerate the learning process and heighten the level of mastery, only exceptional students were recruited. Students entering the program were required to score a minimum of 1100 on the SAT or 25 on the ACT, have an impressive high school transcript, and three strong personal letters of reference. Almost immediately, the five-year M.B.A. began to attract a larger number of students than the traditional M.B.A. degree.

Although the professional M.B.A. was a generalist degree, concentrations were acquired by taking electives in an area of specialty consistent with the students' personal interests. In the highly demanding, competitive program, SBI set and enforced academic retention requirements as well as the required completion of three internships. Students were encouraged accept internships with diverse companies in different geographical areas. Increasingly, internships were international and varied in lengths up to one year.

Thus, the five-year professional M.B.A. as the flagship program was a seamless curriculum with horizontal emphasis across the old silo structure of accounting, finance, marketing, management, and information technology. Requiring a minimum of 155 hours for graduation, the basic curriculum components were: accounting, 15 hours; calculus and physics, 14 hours; required business courses, 40 hours; engineering, 15 hours; business major concentration, 18 hours; professional development, 20 hours; global applications, 9 hours; internships, 3 hours; and general education, 24 hours.

SBI's academic programs provided a sound foundation, preparing students to assume professional positions in national and international organizations. By design, both the undergraduate and graduate programs were competitive, demanding, and rigorous. With a strong liberal education in communications, mathematics, humanities, fine arts, behavioral sciences, social sciences, and natural sciences, students were in a better position to grasp the business content which formed the conceptual foundation of different business functions. Since SBI's academic programs were built on rigor, integrity, and review, from its inception SBI instituted a grading policy to insure the integrity of the grading system. SBI leadership was determined that each grade letter reflect the standards of the most respected business schools in the nation. As a matter of policy, the contents and requirements of courses were reviewed on a continuous basis. Regular classroom activities were reinforced for many years by first a separate SBI library, and in later years, a special SBI library section within the University's structure which housed collections in conformance with all major standard listings of business core collections and reference sources.

As students progressed up the SBI academic ladder, they specialized in areas of concentration (accounting, finance, etc.), taking theoretical and conceptual courses at an intermediate level. The case study method was introduced at the freshman year and continued until the fifth year in an increasing proportion. In the fifth year, students spent at least 60 percent of their time in team-based case study projects. In the midst of their academic preparation, students were required to take intermittent student internships with industrial corporations, public accounting firms, financial institutions, and governmental agencies to gain an understanding of the "real world."

Regardless of the area of specialization, all students in their fourth or fifth year were required to take a capstone course, either an undergraduate or a graduate business policy course. The basic pedagogy of the capstone course was the case study approach in the Harvard tradition. This tradition is changing as SBI develops its case study approach. This final course was an integrative one that brought together all the student had learned in each area at the policy making level. Cases involved decisions ranging from promoting and demoting employees to issues of social responsibility. The booklet, *School of Business: Past and Present. 1970-1980* clearly states:

> Beginning with the basic business core courses, students are constantly reminded that they must master the concepts and analytic skills covered in each course if they are to be able to apply them in their capstone courses. The senior year becomes a most demanding one in which students become literally consumed in the review of previously covered concepts, acquiring deeper understanding, and sharpening their abilities to develop thoughtful approaches, to be effective team members and to provide effective leadership.

In a progressive manner during the four decades of SBI's existence, the curricula have been constantly revised and updated to make certain that SBI's business program is relevant. Throughout Dean Mobley's tenure, the school consistently "raised the bar" academically to assure that it would enroll and graduate students who could meet the changing demands of the corporate world. From the mid-1970s to 1997, SBI focused its attention at the undergraduate level on accounting and business administration. However, during the academic year 1997-1998, and in response to a mandate by the state, SBI established a new 120-credit hour B.S. program, articulated with Florida's community colleges' curricula. The new program was designed to prepare students to meet the needs of firms for professional specialists, and to provide the technical support crucial to special categories of firms. The desired outcome was the development of discipline-oriented curricula that effectively accommodate various demands for professional specialists. Unfortunately, in implementing the new B.S. program, the Leadership Program and professional development of the students was under-emphasized. This lack of emphasis created a notable quality schism between ultra-well prepared five-year M.B.A. students and four-year B.S. students accepted under the State of Florida's mandated articulation agreement with the state's community college system.

SBI continued to support to its one-year M.B.A. program, but special emphasis was placed on its five-year Professional M.B.A. program, which took from the freshman year progressively to the M.B.A. at the end of five years. Not without rancor, divisions of the existing faculty were also created to support the new structure, with both five-year "graduate faculty" and four-year undergraduate faculty.

The student acceptance of the five-year program can be measured by the number of students seeking admission to the five-year program. For example, SBI documents show that of 389 students admitted during the Fall 1996 semester, only five students selected the B.S. program and three transferred to the M.B.A. within two weeks. The goal of the five- year Professional M.B.A. was to produce leaders for the business community. SBI maintained that its high-quality faculty and students, its structure and methodologies, its team teaching and interdisciplinary approach, and its receptive markets all evidenced a high level of success in accommodating talented students and very important markets.

Mobley was extremely proud of SBI's five-year M.B.A. program and provided a rationale and operational pattern for the program in her formal request to the Board of Regents for the establishment of an SBI Center of Excellence (1991). She insisted that the program was developed in response to customer-identified needs that resulted from the following major changes within the business community:

- The emergence of the global business community.
- The explosion of the body of business concepts and knowledge.
- The need for the academic community to assume responsibility for training previously assumed by the business community.
- Changes in the competencies and qualities required for business leadership.

The SBI five-year M.B.A. program:

Accepted students as freshmen for a five-year program. SBI students were enrolled during their sensitive, formative years. Since the value systems and behavior patterns of these teenagers were not yet frozen,

SBI had the opportunity to have a positive impact with reference to those values and qualities that were required for success.

- Immersed students in its (simulated) business culture for five years permitting them to internalize those competencies and behaviors that normally require a long period of "gestation."

- Eliminated the duplication of course requirements (B.S. and M.B.A.) that typify traditional programs. Because of the elimination of this unproductive duplication and the early-on expansion of the student's capacity (via the hi-tech skills development courses) SBI was able to pursue total development. SBI addressed both competencies and content not included in other business programs.

Mobley insisted that the SBI five-year M.B.A. produced highly sophisticated graduates who had developed and honed the skills necessary to meet the challenges of business leadership. In addition, it was cost and time effective since SBI greatly compressed the time required for development. By eliminating the duplication that exists in traditional programs, SBI was able to expand its program to include important offerings not provided in other business programs—e.g., World Cultures, World Resources, Global Logistics I & II, and three engineering courses. Mobley further maintained that: "After graduation, products of traditional programs must seek both professional development and application skills on-the-job, in an environment programmed to eliminate, not develop. Many talented students will be permanently eliminated; however, for those that do survive, it will take eight years for them to catch up with the five-year SBI graduate."

Indeed, the SBI five-year M.B.A. program had unique characteristics in the training process and proved that it was delivering the qualities expected and desired by corporate America. In fact in a May 4, 1997 article in the *St. Petersburg Times* (Florida) entitled "Jobs chase Class of 1997" cited instances of corporate employers from Schering-Plough flying in the fiancé and parents of Anwell Wilbekin, an SBI graduate, from New York to Tallahassee as a graduation present, and other unique recruitment perks provided to SBI students by firms such as Ford Motor Company and Boise Cascade.

Thus, the five-year M.B.A. program was the flagship of the SBI Leadership Program and methodology during the late 1990s and early 2000s. A Doctorate of Business Administration as well as B.S. degrees in Finance, Marketing, and Management Information Systems were proposed prior to Dr. Mobley's retirement in 2003.

Academic programs which have been outlined above comprise just one component of the triumvirate upon which SBI's Leadership Program was built. Professional Development and the Internship Process (the other two components) will be discussed in the next chapter.

5   DESIGNING   A   COMPREHENSIVE PROFESSIONAL DEVELOPMENT PROGRAM

The SBI philosophy of business management training under Dr. Sybil C. Mobley was predicated on the belief that success in the world of business and industry requires both technical and behavioral competencies. Technical competence was achieved primarily through Academic Programs, while behavioral competence was achieved primarily from experiences provided through aspects of the Professional Development (PD) Program. To produce the optimum product—the SBI graduates—both divisions interacted and worked together in pursuit of clearly defined but ever-changing goals and objectives.

Professional Development did not begin as a full-blown, well-defined concept in business training, but emerged mainly from Mobley's increasing understanding of the kind of persons who would likely succeed as managers and leaders in the national and global workforce. As a highly concerned and progressive professor of accounting in the late 1960s, she became thoroughly convinced that FAMU could not produce the quality of graduate that the marketplace demanded through academic preparation alone. Thus, she began to dream of establishing a unique business training program which would provide students with an essential balance of both technical and behavioral competencies. Mobley stated in a Nissan Report (1991): "I've always been convinced that if you're going to produce for the market, you had better first check with the market, and the corporate community is our market." So during the late 1960s and early 1970s, she gained invaluable experience in the corporate market primarily through summer internships.

In encouraging her faculty and students to do internships, she proudly used her internship experiences as examples. She frequently told them: "I've personally worked at Union Carbide, IBM, Chase Manhattan Bank, Price Waterhouse, and the IRS. I had to become comfortable that what I was teaching was relevant to our students' careers. If what we are teaching is not relevant, we attempt to make it so."

Mobley soon convinced selected members of her faculty that behavioral and analytic competencies and skills could best be achieved and made more relevant through a well-defined program in PD, reinforced by a sound internship process. Along with her assistant dean, Thomas H. Lewis, she began to further develop strategy and structure for elements of Professional Development. The formal structure for PD was established and first used with the entering class of 1976.

During 1976 to 1978, PD followed a loosely defined, uncharted course of action in its efforts to provide challenges and experiences designed to develop positive personal qualities among students. Mobley relied heavily upon Lewis who served as her assistant dean from September 1976 to December 1979 when he resigned to become Chief of the Bureau of Housing for the Florida Department of Community Affairs. He held the Master's degree in Urban and Regional Planning from the University of Pittsburgh, and had worked in both Corporate America and governmental services. He soon internalized Mobley's vision for the new non-traditional school. Mobley recalls that Lewis was a "very bright and perceptive young man, and that he and she were always 'on the same page' as they struggled to give structure to her concepts of PD and selective recruiting on the national level."

In an interview with Lewis on May 15, 1998, he recalled how proud he was "to work with this brilliantly gifted person." He stated that Mobley's life "epitomizes what can happen when you have a dream and don't let anyone deter you from realizing your dream." Lewis further declared that Mobley possessed some of the "most unusual persuasive skills that he has witnessed, and a thorough understanding of what black students needed in the business world." Therefore, the interactive methodology of academic programs and professional development for creating behavioral competencies were essential in the training of totally developed graduates for success in corporate America.

In addition to his roles in teaching guidance and counseling, student financial advisement, and recruiting, Lewis appreciated the challenge of working with Mobley in laying a solid foundation for Professional Development. He was tremendously impressed with how effectively students learned essential behavioral skills through the toastmasters (later Orators, Inc.), business writing, speed reading, "close-ups" (small group discussion sessions with corporate executives) with visiting executives, debates, and other learning modalities. One of Lewis' greatest challenges was that of working closely with Mobley in giving structure to the Tuesday forum series in which executives from Fortune 500 companies and from public agencies would serve as speakers. According to Lewis: "As I watched black students from all sections of America rapidly develop in SBI to the point where they could articulate their positions, ask intelligent questions and interact with ease with corporate executives, I really felt blessed that I was able to help Dean Mobley translate her ideas into realities." When Dr. Gloria Rislov was employed in 1978 and charged with the responsibility of more fully developing a formal structure and course work for Professional Development, Lewis turned more of his attention to recruiting high-achieving Superstars for the up- and-coming nationally acclaimed business program.

George Auzenne served subsequently to Lewis as Mobley's assistant dean. He recalled that: "Dean Mobley was one of the most creative and original thinkers that I have ever met. She was an extremely brilliant and resourceful person who could come forth with a half dozen excellent ideas overnight." Auzenne served in several administrative capacities in SBI including the head of the division of Management Science and instructor of Economics during the late *1970's* and 1980s. George R. Auzenne died in September 2003, just after Mobley's retirement.

Mobley's unique ideas for improving the quality of business training for her students was not well-received initially by the academic Deans' Council at FAMU, nor by many other colleges and universities across the nation which adhered to traditional patterns of business training. The Academic Deans' Council argued vehemently that professional development activities, which were not purely academic in nature, ciphered much-needed funds away from established academic, credit-bearing courses. At best, the Council maintained that Professional Development should be merely supplemental programmatic activities carried out through existing academic courses. Several administrators at FAMU; leaders in business programs at other colleges and schools; and even the Association to Advance Collegiate Schools of Business (AACSB), a major accrediting body for business schools; initially considered Professional Development a purely technical program which should be more appropriately associated with community colleges.

Despite the doubts and initial criticisms, Mobley and her faculty were not dissuaded from pursuing an idea in business education whose time had come. She was convinced that technical competence and behavioral competence were essential for success in the business world, and that an organized, and structured training in a Professional Development Program was the best way to help students achieve appropriate behavioral and problem-solving competence. Within a five-year period, Mobley's idea had caught the attention of the corporate world, and FAMU's business program had become the envy of many other colleges and universities. Looking back on the historic development of SBI, Mary Christine Phillips writing in *Black Issues in Higher Education* (September 8, 1994) said: "The school's innovative approach to business education has won for it a reputation as one of the best in the nation when it comes to preparing business leaders and managers, and that's particularly appealing to recruiters and CEOs from Fortune 500 companies." Additionally, Don Wilson, Director of Staffing, Amoco Corporation of Chicago said: "The quality of the program is focused on preparing students on how to apply what they've learned in the classrooms to the real business world."

One might ask why was Mobley so insistent upon establishing a Professional Development Program that she believed would fully prepare students for business careers. She once gave the following answer: "We went to firms and asked, 'What is it you're not satisfied with [respect to] college graduates?' The responses from the companies were nearly unanimous: "While college students usually possessed the technical competence to perform entry-level work, they frequently lack the discipline and aggressiveness that are required for superior achievement" (*Newsweek*, May 24, 1982). Being thoroughly convinced of the needs of the corporate world, Mobley conceived and originated a "total development" plan that combined the traditional emphasis on academic programs with a professional development program designed to impose a business-like structure on the school environment. The result was an innovative approach to business education that won the plaudits of many corporations and business schools throughout the nation.

The overall purpose of PD, as stated in SBI published documents was "to provide business professionals with a high degree of communication, skills, business sophistication and positive personal qualities." Thus, opportunities were provided for each student to develop: (1) A high degree of interpersonal skills; (2) An intense awareness of current developments in the business world; and, (3) An ability to apply techniques to goal achievement with shifting contextual demands, in short, the use of judgment.

As stated earlier, Dr. Gloria R. Rislov, Ph.D. from Wayne University arrived at SBI for the 1978-1979 academic year and as the designated leader of the program was responsible for much of the initial formal coursework for Professional Development. It was under her administration that the initial implementation of many aspects of the new concept took shape. Looking back on her organizational work, she stated in the *National Black Monitor* (March, 1981) that SBI's array of professional development activities was unique in business education. Through the program she maintained that: "SBI has found that there is much that can be done in the school setting to permit students to better understand and function in a business environment." During the early stages amid trepidation and anxiety amongst PD staff, a unique program was born in the preparation of business students. However it was under Dr. Norman Johnson and Dr. Amos H. Bradford that professional Development became a viable program in the curriculum.

This school means business

Freshman Annette Singleton, attending SBI on a scholarship, says she feels the school's internship program gives her a distinct advantage over students attending other business schools.

(excerpt from SBI Recruitment brochure: Permission granted. September/October 1986 issue of Amoco Torch Magazine)

The Professional Development curriculum was not contained within the traditional classroom setting. Rather, it was an experienced-based curriculum which consisted of a series of planned activities which stressed confidence building, oral communications, business writing (formerly Magic Pen), goal-setting planning, results-orientation, and the dynamics of functioning as part of a business team. The long time chair of the Division of Professional Development, Dr. Amos H. Bradford (retired as an Associate Professor in 2013) explained the program in a Nissan Report (1991) in this manner. "What we've developed and continue to develop is a process for developing a number of business competencies. The cumulative effects of the process make the difference and allow our students to be successful."

Structurally, during the early years, the student body of SBI was organized into different mock companies. Under the conglomerate of SBI Companies, Inc. with its Chairman of the Board, Chief Program Auditor, vice Chairman, Executive Committee and Board of Directors, at least seven other companies were then in operation. As the years went by, the above structure was changed and companies increased to make PD conform more to the needs of SBI students and still maintain a business-like environment.

By 1981 the student-operated companies were: Diversified Labs, Inc. which focused on forum, Close-ups, Social Labs and Health Labs; Communications, Inc.—WSBI, Publications and Graphic Displays; Services, Inc.—Escort/Tours, transportation, and Photography; Management Development, Inc.—Human Resource Management, Training and Certification; Property Management, Inc.—Maintenance Division, Social Division Operations, Security and Safety, and Finance and Operations; and Surety Agency, Inc.—Sales, Personnel, Marketing and Corporate Development. Each of the above mock companies was presided over by a CEO, and each division was headed by a president. Operating beneath each president was a cadre of managers, supervisors, and operating staff. Students, guided by faculty and staff advisors were largely responsible for the operational duties required for each firm.

By 1990, the number of student firms had expanded as well as the structure. The student companies had been expanded and essential changes had been made to accommodate an increasing number of business students and to take into account the technical and behavioral changes simultaneously taking place in the corporate world. Dr. Bradford emphasized the importance of the firm structure in an interview when he said: "in the mock companies, we reinforce organizational skills and teach students how to develop strategies and realize business objectives." He further explained that "it's a real-time, action-oriented environment that gives students opportunities to practice the entire set of skills they'll need in the workplace."

Bradford worked effectively with Dean Mobley in his efforts to develop a well-prepared, experienced faculty with significant credible experience in the business world to carry out the overall purpose of Professional Development. The PD faculty consisted both of tenure-earning members most of whom held earned doctorates in their fields, and others with extensive corporate experience and masters degrees or the Masters in Business Administration who held ranks of Associates/Assistants in Professional Development on non-tenured tracks. The appropriately credentialed faculty not only taught and prepared the companies' individual curriculums, but they also were encouraged to participate in faculty internships or "consultantships" themselves and engaged in research designed to keep Professional Development abreast of the changes and needs of the corporate world. They experienced tremendous success in preparing SBI students with the behavioral and application competencies essential for upward mobility in the field of business.

In 1991, Dr. Amos Bradford labeled the program as "an influence model"—meaning the acquisition of the desired skills and competencies that allow for greater ability to persuade and influence others in a business environment. The model encouraged the effective combination of skills, knowledge, acquisition, and application from the freshman year until the completion of the degree program.

Although Professional Development included many of the same components and used some of the same methodologies as it did during the beginning years, in 1990, changes were made to the program, allowing it to become more clearly defined and articulated. The following Professional Development Requirements (based on the five-year M.B.A. program) reveal the increased strengths and expanded patterns during the 1990s:

Five-Year M.B.A. Program
Professional Development Course Requirements[1]

YEAR ONE (First Semester)
GEB1931
    Survey
    IRA
    Orators
    Forum
    Freshman Training
    Company Assignment[2]

YEAR ONE (Second Semester)
GEB 1932
    TRA
    Business writing
    Forum
    Freshman Training
    Company Assignment

YEAR TWO (First Semester)
GEB 2931
    Close-Up
    Social Labs (receptions)
    Forum
    Business Writing
    Company Assignment

YEAR TWO (Second Semester)
GEB 2932
    Close-Up
    Social labs
    Orators
    Forum
    Company Assignment

YEAR THREE (First Semester)
GEB 3931
    Close-Up
    Social Labs
    Business Writing
    Forum
    Company Assignment

YEAR THREE(Second Semester)
GEB 3932
    Close-Up
    Social labs
    Orators
    Forum
    Company Assignment

Graduate Level, Five Year M.B.A.

YEAR FOUR (First Semester)
Without Business Sport

GEB 5931
    Senior Seminar Series

YEAR FOUR(Second Semester)
Without Business Sport

GEB 5932
    Senior Seminar Series

---

[1] Nine sequential courses are required.
[2] All Company Assignments are level and Grade Point Average sensitive.

TV Taping	TV Taping
Forum	Forum
Social Labs (receptions, luncheons, & dinners)	Social Labs
Close-Up	Company Assignment

YEAR FIVE (First Semester)   YEAR FIVE (second semester)

GEB 5933	GEB 5934
Forum	Forum
Grad Close-Up & Social Labs	Grad Close-Up and Social Labs
Topical Seminars	Topical Seminars
Teaching or Company Assignment	Teaching or Company Assignment

ONE YEAR MBA   ONE YEAR MBA
(First Semester)   (Second Semester)

GEB 5933	GEB 5934
Survey[3]	Grad Close-Up & Social Labs
Grad Close-Up & Social Labs	Forum
Forum	Company Assignment
Company Assignments	

Each of the Professional Development courses contained a set of learning objectives. The published course objectives for the SBI freshman (1995) year were (1) to speak with confidence about current business issues; (2) to develop and enhance articulation and memory skills; (3) to demonstrate leadership behaviors and characteristics; and (4) to develop oratory excellence, poise, and a sense of competitiveness.

At the outset of the developmental process, freshman and new SBI students began with the introductory PD course, GEB 1931. This course included a five-week orientation component, Survey, which reviewed the unique SBI culture, the pitfalls of the student's status and corporate, the judicious use of time, and entry-level, business-related, industry skills.

As freshmen took the Professional Development courses GEB 1931 and GEB 1932, they engaged in a variety of enriching experiences designed to acquaint them with the demands of the

---

[3] Exemptions might apply

business world while at the same time bonding with each other, their classmates. Among the experiences were Information Review and analysis (IRA) and Technology Review and analysis (TRA) components which served as introduction to business-oriented research. Students became familiar with databases, the industry lexicon, and the various titles that are essential to the analysis of current events in the business world. *Value Line*, *Moody's Index*, *Fortune*, *Business Week*, *Black Enterprise*, and the *Wall Street Journal* were just a few of the resources SBI students learned to use. The goal was to instill in students that investigation and awareness of major business trends should become second nature to them during the early stages of their training.

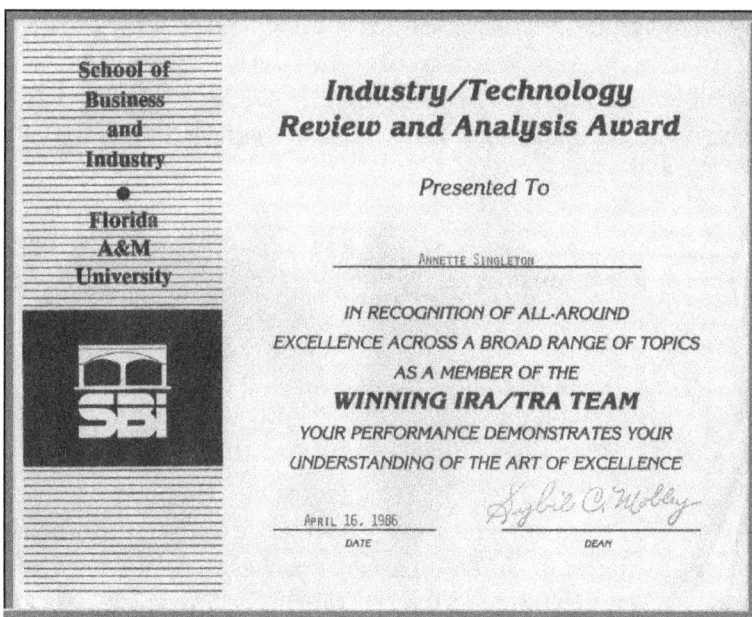

In other communication components, freshman students were also required to be involved in such companies as Orators, Business Writing, and Freshman Training. While some student participants of these companies remained in the same companies throughout several academic years, the requirements became more demanding and intense as students progressed from one academic level to another. The faculty for a given area prepared the companies' individual curriculum and directed students in pursuit of the desired competencies. In order to give readers a better understanding of the developmental process, an example is provided through a detailed description of the competencies of Orators, Inc. Orators Club (as it was initially called), was one of the beginning companies in 1976 with Thomas H. Lewis as its leader. Orators, Inc. was variously under the guidance of Dr. Gloria Rislov, Jean Lambert, Doris D. Corbett, and Dr. Gail Thompkins, each of whom made contributions to its developmental history. In its form prior to the retirement of Dean Mobley, it was under the leadership of Dr. Vera J. Harper (retired, 2013) who further expanded the list of competencies.

Orators, Inc. according to early SBI documents, was designed to help students overcome any mechanical problems they might have had standing before an audience and presenting information; to enhance the students' ability to effectively present information; and raise students' consciousness to the reality that presenter is responsible for the quality of his or her presentation. Harper explained the competencies and explanations in a 1998 interview as follows:

FRESHMEN

At the freshman level, students are expected to master these competencies:

Dependability	Oral Communication
Written Communication	Analytical Ability
Critical Thinking	Responsibility

These competencies were developed through Impromptu Speaking, Recitations, and Prepared Speeches. The ultimate test of mastery was demonstrated at the Freshman Oratorical Contest.

SOPHOMORES

Students at the sophomore level are expected to master those competencies identified at the freshman level as well as these:

Managerial Skills	Accountability	Teamwork

These competencies were developed and mastered through Impromptu Speaking, Prepared Speeches, Interpersonal Communication, and Resume Writing/Interview Techniques. The final activity for these students was the Oratorical Debate. This debate put the best of the best of the team members against the best of the junior class.

JUNIORS

The junior year culminated the Orators training for SBI students. The junior curriculum included training in Impromptu Speaking, Prepared Speeches, Resume Writing/Interview Skills, Individual and Group Presentations, and Oratorical Debate against the sophomore class. Students were expected to demonstrate that they had developed and mastered these competencies:

Accountability.	Managerial Skills
Analytical Ability	Oral Communication
Critical Thinking	Responsibility
Dependability	Team Work
Leadership	Written Communication

The above component, Orators, Inc., shows the purposes, aims, and the expected competencies that students were expected to master at different levels. Each of the twenty-three companies had similar outlines and expected competencies; however, space does not permit the writer to describe each of them in as much detail. It should be noted that some companies were a part of regular formal classroom activities (i.e. Orators and Business Writing) while performance, service, and entrepreneurial companies gained their experiences outside the normal classroom.

Business Writing, Inc., which was an expanded version of what was originally called "Magic Pen," is another of the communication components. This component focused on the ability to present ideas coherently in written form. Students were provided with opportunities to polish their English Skills, learn basic business formats, and produce similar documents themselves. During early years, SBI wrote in its published literature that Business Writing was designed to: (a) Help students overcome any mechanical problems they may have in presenting information in the written form; (b) Enhance the students' ability to effectively present information; and (c) Sensitize students to the importance of the visual impact of written work. The curriculum was designed to help students keep up with new and evolving trends in business.

Freshman Training was also a corner of the communications block. It was peer-based in its delivery, and aimed to provide the student experience in business etiquette. This course focused on the finer points of business dress, business meals and entertainment, and methods of presenting oneself. It helped the student coordinate and assimilate the variety of learning experiences that they had during the first year at SBI. This component was especially needed to help students feel confident in business settings, which may contain a quagmire of unspoken etiquette pitfalls formerly unknown to uninitiated entry-level workers.

Professional Development also provided valuable business training for students through four performance companies: Close-Up, Forum, Social Labs, and WSBI. Through these companies, students were given an opportunity to practice what they learned in their communication companies. A brief overview of each performance company will be shown below:

Close-Up, Inc.—In this company students were required to engage corporate executives in a face to face setting. This was a relatively intimate setting that included up to twenty-five students around the boardroom table engaging in meaningful dialogue with a corporation representative. Not only were questions encouraged, but also the sharing of ideas and observations. Close-Ups further provided opportunities for students to gauge the level of communication skills they had achieved and also the level of business concepts acquired and their ability to relate those concepts to the issues and challenges of the particular firm. Student officers of Close-Up, Inc. evaluated the performance of lower level students and counseled them in ways to improve the appropriateness of their interaction with representatives from business and government.

Though it differs in various ways from Mobley-era forum, the main idea of SBI Forum remains present in today's SBI. SBI Forum is different from the Close-up experience in that the guest presents a major address to the entire student body in an auditorium setting. Following the address, students ask questions prompted by the address. All questions must be timely, relevant and precisely stated. The students' questions and answers provide faculty and corporate guests opportunities to evaluate the understanding of academically related concepts, students' analysis and application of those concepts as well as an array of personal skills—ability to think and speak on one's feet and the ability to form relevant questions. Due to the close-knit Sanctuary-style environment, SBI popular culture includes myriad inside jokes spawned from the fodder of the forum question and answer period—some questions and students—reaching legendary SBI status.

Social Labs, Inc.—These companies provided opportunities for students to interact with business representatives in a variety of settings away from the university at social activities such as corporate recruiting receptions, luncheons, and dinners. These activities called for students to apply all they had learned in freshman training (business dress, etiquette, etc.), in Professional Development, and in academic courses. The Social Labs provided invaluable performance opportunities for SBI students.

WSBI, Inc.—This was the fourth and final performance company. WSBI encompassed the SBI Television Studio which was student-driven and equipped with state-of-the-art facilities. Here students interviewed and recorded their interaction with corporate executives. Students' prepared questions resulted in an interview program that documented the visits and the students' performance for the SBI records. Many corporate CEOs over the years commented on the nature of these interviews—many stating that they had felt more on the "hot seat" at SBI than on prominent business news shows of the day, e.g. MacNeil/Lehrer News Hour.

Professional Development had eleven Service Companies, which provided just what their titles imply—service. SBI News, Inc., for example, created a newsletter, providing background information on visiting corporate executives, their particular corporations, and an industry review. This document was entitled, *SBI profile*. Written by students, it was produced for every Forum. Services, Inc. provided a student escort for visiting cooperative executives and other dignitaries. They met the visitors at the airport, took them to their hotels, escorted them through the SBI building, and accompanied them throughout the day. The Service Companies provided that special touch during corporate visits and student campus visits that differentiated the SBI experience from most other business schools.

The last company was comprised of the entrepreneurial companies which provided insurance and investment experiences for students under the aegis of Surety, Inc. The development of entrepreneurial skills was vital to the functioning of SBI. Therefore it was at Surety that students learned the meaning of self-determination first-hand. Success in these companies was dependent upon knowledge, application of skills, and work ethic combined with sound judgment.

SBI students' professional development and academic training were field tested and further developed during student internships, a firm requirement during Dr. Mobley's era. Always germane to internship discussions, were Dean Mobley's personal internship/consulting experiences at Union Carbide, IBM, Chase Manhattan Bank, Price Waterhouse, and the Internal Revenue Service.

Both student and faculty internships were administered by Ms. Faye Williams through the SBI Internship Office. Subsequent to a reorganization of the department, it was named the Office of Recruitment, Admissions, Internships and Prep-schools and was led by Ms. Doris Corbett, a transfer from the professional development staff in 1993. Some of her early hires were SBI Superstars. Corbett calls the internship office of the early 1990's a Ph.D. development lab. Several SBI graduates, trying to decide on a career in academia used it to "get their feet wet" including Seralyn Pink, and Laquita Blockson. Corbett also directed SBI recruiting from her office for which Ed Knox and later O'Hara Hannah were responsible. H.B. Pinkney, Ph.D. also joined the internship office staff as coordinator of the prep-school program. Doris Corbett retired from SBI in 2010 as the Director of the SBI Department of Corporate Relationships and Alumni Affairs.

In an interview with Doris Corbett, she described her 1993 arrival in the internship office, which was subsequent to the departure of the previous director, Faye Williams:

> We were a small department. It was an overwhelming task to get all the students placed and all the paperwork done for all of the recruiting, admissions, internships, faculty internships, and office functions. Additionally, I got my marching orders from the Dean who wanted more international internship placements.

Behavioral as well as content competence was stressed in awarding internships to students. In addition to coursework completed and grade point averages, Internship Office staff also used a unique SBI leadership quotient to determine internship placement.

This quotient was based on students' professional development performance and the recommendation of faculty and staff members.

Students were encouraged to accept internships with diverse companies in different geographical areas. Though, in special cases, students were allowed multiple internships at the same company or to accept internships in the same geographical area. A very successful recruiting tool for Mobley, students were required at various times throughout the history of the program to have between one and three internships. Unlike the standard of student cooperatives at the time, Mobley's student interns were highly-prized and well paid.

Between the 1980's and Mobley's retirement, School of Business and Industry internal documents list thousands of student interns at Fortune 500 companies. Of particular note is the list of "Global Residency Sites" which detail hundreds of international internship placements in Europe (Belgium, England, France, Germany, Italy, Netherlands, Russia, Spain); Africa (Egypt, Kenya, Madagascar, Morocco, Nigeria, South Africa); Asia (China, India, Japan, Korea, Indonesia); Central America (El Salvador, Honduras, Panama); South America (Brazil, Chile); the Caribbean (British Virgin Islands, Jamaica, Trinidad, Virgin Islands); and The Middle East (Israel, Saudi Arabia) in marketing and sales, accounting, finance, logistics, human resources, and management. It is clear that Corbett hit the mark in placing students with firms everywhere in the world.

Similar to the other ground-breaking areas within Sybil Mobley's School of Business and Industry, the internship program was also touted in the media as something very special. In fact, an April 18, 1990 article in *The New York Times* entitled "Modest University in Florida Is Blazing a Trail for Blacks to Careers in the World of Business" corporate executives extol the virtues of the internship program as key in the development of several highly-sought business school graduates. Another article in the May 17, 1987 *St. Petersburg Times*, "Students see their future at FAMU" also discusses several SBI students and internship experiences including SBI Senior Roy Washington's internships at Monsanto and Dow Chemical; and SBI's Reginald Mitchell's assertion that an SBI internship "not only taught him business skills, it also taught him how to survive independently."

Appropriate to the huge role played by internships in the professional development of SBI students, any response by an SBIan to a question about their years at the school are inexorably linked to their internship experiences as students. Students with internships in New York City, Boston, and Philadelphia often found themselves in urban environments with multiple fellow SBIans interning with various Fortune 500 companies—another bonding opportunity to reinforce SBI's sanctuary effect. Anecdotally, as a Sales Training consultant to GlaxoSmithKline, in the summer of 2001, SBI professor Annette Singleton (Jackson) arrived in Philadelphia to find 23 SBI students interns with the Fortune 500 pharmaceutical giant. Singleton requested a meeting with the 16 SBI interns in the area.

This created an opportunity for Singleton to introduce a few of the students to the Vice President of Vaccine Sales and the President of Marketing. Due to the spontaneous nature of the meeting, it was not possible to separate the SBI students from several other students in the training class for the initial, impromptu meeting. The opportunity turned into a WOW moment for the executives and a teaching moment for the other, non-FAMU students. In characteristic SBI Superstar style, the FAMU students gave the standard SBI handshake and gave the standard SBI introduction to the very impressed executives. "Hello, I am Nicole Ricketts, a Senior Business Administration major from Houston Texas. My internship experiences include financial analysis at Marriott International, and marketing and public relations at Nike." As Tallahassee radio personality and voice of the Florida A&M University Marching 100 would say, "The difference was clear."

6 THE DIFFERENCE IS CLEAR

Professional Development and internship requirements both formally served as an invaluable part of SBI's Leadership Program since 1974, and have provided behavioral competence for several thousand graduates who have found employment in corporate America and elsewhere. One of the best ways to evaluate the impact of the program in the overall business education process of students is to interview graduates who have successfully completed the program and have entered the world of work.

Keith Clinkscales ('86), formerly Senior Vice President and General Manager at ESPN, President and CEO at Vibe/Spin Ventures, Chairman and CEO at Vangaurde Media, now serves as the CEO at REVOLT Media & TV, stated in a 2012 interview:

> The most important lesson I learned from SBI was the idea that if I worked hard in the program, I would then be prepared for the modern business world. Dean Mobley repeated to us constantly that we were "Superstars" and SBI would make us better, that affirmation provided me with confidence and more importantly culture awareness.
>
> I felt that Professional Development was an exceptional program that exposed me to the world of organizations, meetings and attending business functions. Culminating with the weekly forums, close-up and television tapings gave me personal and up close interaction with a number of key business people. Today, I still interface with several of those that I met on the SBI campus. Professional development is especially important for African American

students because it provides a unique opportunity to interact in a professional manner while still learning the new world of business. In short, professional development provides you with a foundation for your career, the ropes to skip... and the ropes to know.

SBI taught me to be persistent. SBI also taught me to demand more of myself at all times and to know that there was nothing that I could not do. My time at FAMU was in NO way an impediment for the real world. An "A" at Florida A&M was an "A" anywhere... I heard that when I was in school, but I believed it as I began to grow in my ambition and accomplishments.

The SBI network is strong, and anytime I hear from a classmate of mine who walked Lee Hall with me and over to the new SBI Building, it is just like we just walked off of campus. The network of achievement is substantial, and the respect that is garnered from others has been exceptional

Jeff Moore ('86) made this comment with reference to Professional Development and what it did for him:

> As freshmen, I think we were all resentful of all the work, the total immersion in business culture. From the moment you get on campus you hit the ground running. Then, one day you wake up and you realize that all of it has become a part of you. It's not homework to watch Nightly Business Report on TV or to read *The Wall Street Journal.* You do it because you want to do it instinctively." (AMOCO Torch, September/October, 1986).

John A. Hardy ('89), former Group Purchasing Manager Procter and Gamble Company, now serves as the Sourcing Expert for Digital & Mobile Marketing at The Coca-Cola Company. In an interview on April 3, 1998, he gave accolades to the Professional Development program:

> Helping me to gain confidence in myself; for providing opportunities to learn and use the language of the business world; for the repetition of interacting with corporate

executives; and for the overall professionalism that is so essential for success in the corporate community. My experiences from Professional Development and internships gave me an organizational understanding and practical outlook on the corporate world that placed me on par with M.B.A.s. It really helped me to become exposed to and function effectively in the business culture.

Andrew N. Lewis, III ('83), Former Vice President and Senior Private Banker, Northern Trust states:

My FAMU 'SBI' (School Of Business And Industry) experience was sensational! The speaking, writing, interviewing, and etiquette training was special and unique. It gave me the confidence to take on Corporate America. I had the privilege to work directly with Dr. Sybil C. Mobley (a legend!) on various SBI projects. The work habits that Dr. Mobley and SBI instilled in us were invaluable. It was great learning from the best! While flying to Chicago for an internship, I befriended the singing group Sister Sledge. After talking with Kathy Sledge (the lead singer), she invited me to be their special guest at a Park West concert in Chicago. Remember SBI Orator's Class? Well, I gave impromptu speaking a new meaning on that airplane! (2012)

Sonya J. Myles ('89), former Manager, Ford College Graduate training Program for Purchasing, Ford Automotive Operations, Dearborn, Michigan had nothing but praise for the Professional Development program during an interview on April 3, 1998. She stated emphatically:

Attending FAMU (and SBI) was the single most important decision in my life. Specifically, Professional Development provided me. with a variety of behavioral competencies which enabled me to make a great impression on management. As president of Social labs, Inc. at SBI, I learned the value of planning, to juggle schedules, to manage people, to manage conflict resolution, and to interact frequently with representatives from companies in a variety of settings. Thus,

I did not feel intimidated upon entering a corporate environment where one is expected to ask questions and communicate effectively, both verbally and in business writing. Having been exposed all of the facets of Professional Development; I left SBI feeling that I had the 'total package' for success in corporate America. I noticed that students from other business schools were generally playing 'catch up' to SBIans whose academic, technical, and behavioral training had prepared them for a variety of pursuits in industry.

Additionally, more of an unheralded achievement of the SBIans is the successful pursuit of terminal degrees by SBIans. Though there is no formal count, there are many SBIans who hold the Ph.D. in business. This is no minor accomplishment in view of the fact that less than 1% of African-Americans hold Ph.D.s. In fact, several SBIans with the Ph.D. in currently serve on the SBI faculty including the current Dean, Shawnta Friday-Stroud, Ph.D. (1997, Florida International University), Kelley Bailey, Ph.D. (2010, Florida A&M University), Michael Campbell (2001, Nova Southeastern University), Atira Charles, Ph.D. (2009, Arizona State University), Saundra Twiggs Drumming, Ph.D. (1982, University of Wisconsin), Roscoe Hightower, Jr., Ph.D. (1997, Florida State University), Angela Murphy, Ph.D. (2001, Case Western Reserve University), and Annette Singleton Jackson, Ph.D. (2002, Florida State University).

There are also countless SBIans currently on the faculties of various business schools across the country. A non-exhaustive list includes Erinn Tucker Ph.D. at Boston University; Verina Mathis-Crawford at Baruch College; Frank Bryant Ph.D. at California State Polytechnic University at Pomona; Alfred "Reedy" Smith, Ph.D. at Johnson C. Smith University; Karen Proudford, Ph.D. at Morgan State University; Wanda Lester, Ph.D., Vice Provost, North Carolina A&T University; Cynthia Miree-Coppin, Ph.D. at Oakland University; Sharon D. James, Ph.D. at Ohio State University; Michelle Harris at Paine College; Janee' Burkhalter, Ph.D. at St. Joseph's University; Laquita Blockson, Ph.D. at St. Leo University; Alisa Mosley, Ph.D., Vice President for Academic Affairs, Tennesee State University; Olenda Johnson, Ph.D. at the U.S. Naval War College; John L. Green, Ph.D. at University of Houston; T. Nicole Phillips at the University of Mary Washington; Wendy Walker,

University of North Georgia; Brandie Franklin, Ph.D. at the University of Tennesee; Gail Dawson, Ph.D. at University of Tennessee Chattanooga; and Doria Kathy Stitts, Ph.D. at Winston-Salem State University. There are also several SBIans currently in the Ph.D. pipeline including Yvette Holmes at Florida State University and Randall Croom at the University of Florida.

Another measure of accomplishment is the extent to which the program is preparing students to meet the demands of an ever changing business community. For example, the American Accounting Association indicated in the *New Accountant* (September, 1991) that future accountants were, not being prepared properly to meet the demands of the expansive and more complex procession that is emerging. It states: "As faculty have attempted to cram more and more facts into the curriculum, time spent developing a conceptual understanding of accounting and information and improving intellectual, interpersonal and communication skills have diminished. Apparently, the above criticism does not apply to SBI. Since the mid-1960s FAMU has concentrated its efforts on developing appropriate business and interpersonal skills at all academic levels. In the *New Accountant*, (September, 1991) the same article stated that "corporate recruiters complain that M.B.A.s lack creativity, people skills, aptitude for teamwork, and the ability to speak and write with clarity and conciseness—all hallmarks of a good manager." While the corporate world may deride the process of course proliferation in certain business disciplines, and chastise business schools for turning out M.B.A. graduates who lack interpersonal and behavioral competencies, SBI has not failed in those areas. The five-year M.B.A. program requires professional development training from the freshman year through the fifth year. An article in the September/October 1986 issue of the *Amoco Torch*, Richard M. Morrow, Chairman of Amoco Corporation, speaking of SBI graduates said:

> ...the graduates from this largely rural, agricultural school in Tallahassee are among the most sought after by corporate recruiters nationwide. The reasons have to do with their knowledge of the corporate world and their tuned-in business sense." He further praised SBI students for their "communication skills—both verbally and in writing.

Glowing praise for Professional Development has come from scholars in the field after a thorough examination of all SBI academic and professional programs. In 1984, just ten years after SBI was established, the Board of Regents' program Review teams made thorough evaluation of all business schools in the State University system. The Review team which evaluated SBI made this statement in regard to its Professional Development Program:

> The professional development program is unique and might well serve as a model for all schools of business. It involves all students in internships, oral and written presentations to peers with evaluation by peers, familiarity with business executives from "Fortune 500" companies, and practices in the social graces. It appears to develop personal, non-cognitive skills to a remarkable degree and competencies few programs can match. The program is unique in its strength of its preparations for interpersonal and other management and skills and personal characteristics.

There is substantial evidence that many prestigious schools of business throughout America have adopted many aspects of SBI's program for which seeds were planted as early as the 1960s and consistently upgraded and expanded during the 1970s and thereafter. A quick search of the internet will yield hundreds of business schools that now contain once controversial professional development components. In considering a major overhaul of its M.B.A. program Wharton indicated that their changes: (1) place greater emphasis on people skills, (2) add more global prospective, (3) foster creativity and innovation, (4) promote real-world problem-solving and (5) examine business issues from the viewpoint of several disciplines. (*Business Week*, May 13, 1991).

In many respects, three of the above changes announced by Wharton in 1991 follow directly in the programmatic patterns which have been in effect at SBI for more than twenty-three years at both the baccalaureate and M.B.A. levels. However, SBI's affect on academia goes farther than the now pervasive Professional Development content and the many SBIans on business school faculties around the country. Indeed, many of the faculty and administrators trained by Dr. Mobley within SBI have gone on to be Deans of business schools. Former SBI faculty members have gone on to lead business schools at many institutions including Alabama State University, Bethune-Cookman University, Florida State University, Fort Valley State University, Hampton University, North Carolina A&T University, South Carolina State University, Syracuse University, Texas Southern University, Tuskegee University, and the University of the District of Columbia.

From its early beginnings, SBI sought to impose a business-like structure on the school environment. To achieve this goal, students were divided into functioning miniature corporations, with upperclassmen serving as CEOs and top managers. From the freshman year through the five-year M.B.A. program, students engaged in intensive activities designed to enhance both oral and written communication; participated in forums and social laboratories which permitted interaction with visiting executives; participated in group discussions on books and delivered planned and impromptu speeches on business; and operated in improvised business settings. While at school, SBI Superstars were immersed, sanctuary-style in business—all day, every day. They were competitive, but also very close-knit and collegial. Along with the academic and professional development programs, students were assigned to a variety of internships in major corporations or public agencies. The overall aim of the Leadership Program, of which Professional Development is a component, was to send to corporate America thoroughly equipped students with the "total package" for successful work and service.

Businesses immediately recognized the value of Dean Mobley's Superstars and continue to pursue, promote, and retain thousands of members of THE FORCE.

Almost forty years after its inception, SBI Superstars infiltrate every nook and cranny of the Fortune 500, entrepreneurial concerns, industry as a whole, education, education administration, and whatever area we have chosen to try our hands.

Indeed, Business Education, corporate America, and the world will never be the same. It appears Dean Sybil C. Mobley, PhD, definitely got it right.

Long live SBI.

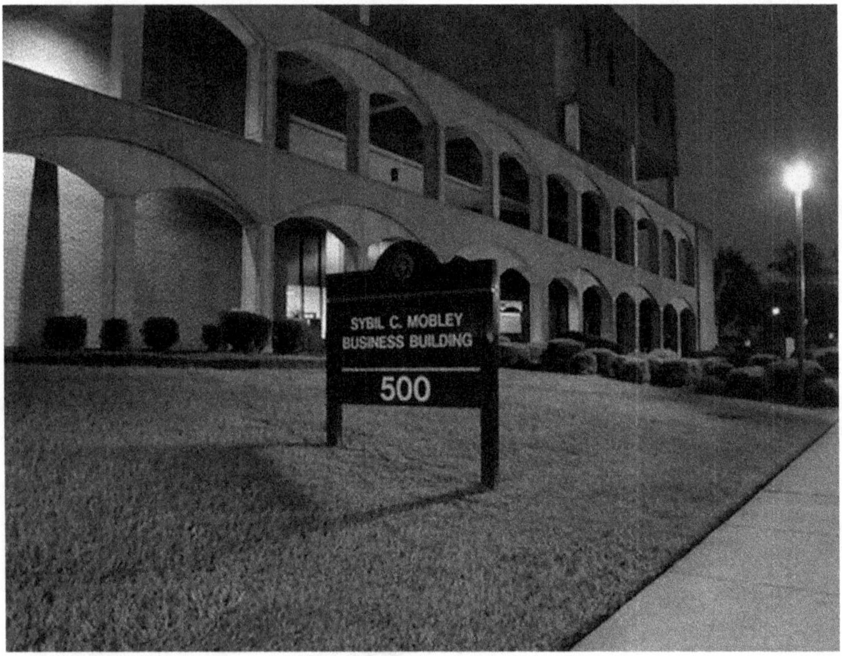
SYBIL C. MOBLEY
BUSINESS BUILDING
500

ABOUT THE AUTHORS

Dr. Annette Singleton Jackson is an Associate Professor of Marketing at the School of Business and Industry at Florida A&M University. She holds a B.S. in Economics with a minor in Business Administration from Florida A&M University (1989), and a Ph.D. in Marketing with a support area of Communication from The Florida State University (2002). Dr. Jackson is an avid participant in community service, and a Diamond Life Member of Delta Sigma Theta Sorority, Inc. initiated at Florida A&M University through the Beta Alpha Chapter in the Fall of 1986. She is also a Life Member of Jack and Jill of America, a Life Member of Florida A&M University National Alumni Association, and a Life Member of The Florida State University Alumni Association.

Annette is married to Dr. E. Newton Jackson, Jr. and has two children. Adrianne is a graduate of Florida State University (2011). Edgar, III is a 1st grader and a champion at spelling.

◉

Dr. Leedell W. Neyland, Professor Emeritus, retired as the Provost and Vice President of Academic Affairs at Florida AM University after a long, distinguished career as historian, author, and department chair of History, and Dean of the College of Arts and Sciences. He is a member of Sigma Pi Phi Fraternity, Phi Beta Sigma Fraternity, and has a long list of leadership positions, accolades, publications, awards, and honors.

www.ingramcontent.com/pod-product-compliance
Lightning Source LLC
Chambersburg PA
CBHW071607200326
41519CB00021BB/6910